CW01623362

Confessions of a BnB Owner

Steve Fullwood

RAVEN CREST

BOOKS

Publishing the best in new literary voices

www.ravencrestbooks.com
www.ravencrestbooks.co.uk

Copyright © 2018 Steve Fullwood

The right of Steve Fullwood to be identified as the author of this work has been asserted by him in accordance with the Copyright, Designs and Patents Act 1988

All rights reserved.

Some names and identifying details have been changed to protect the privacy of individuals.

No part of this publication may be reproduced, stored in a retrieval system or transmitted in any form or by any means including photocopying, electronic, recording or otherwise, without the prior written permission of the rights holder, application for which must be made through the publisher.

ISBN-13: 978-1-9997803-7-1

INTRODUCTION

When Jane and I started our bed and breakfast in 2013 a good friend of mine said that I should make a note of all the things that happened here. I think he thought it would be a cross between *Fawlty Towers* and *Confessions of a Window Cleaner*. This book is littered with stories about guests and the experiences we have had whilst running our little business but none of the stories are what we might have anticipated. There is nothing salacious and despite being a little eccentric I have never frogmarched through the breakfast room. What we did discover was that we had embarked on an anthropological experiment that we had never anticipated.

Over the five years we have been running Marlow House BnB we have met over 3500 people of all ages from all over the world and all walks of life. It has been enlightening, hilarious and at times genuinely surprising. Like so many new businesses, we have learnt on the job, made mistakes and stumbled upon some unexpected successes. This book is a compilation of all those things.

Mixed in with the stories and observations are some very useful tips if you are considering opening your own BnB or small hotel; from the smallest details of making a popular breakfast to dealing with the biggest online travel agents in the world. I have tried to cover every aspect of the business from dealing with your local council, understanding how VAT works to dealing with difficult guests.

If you are considering a career change, something to do in semi-retirement or as we did, stumble into it by rattling around in a big house then this is a must read. Hopefully by the end you will have a pretty good idea of what is entailed and what you might come up against. It's not for everyone but for those who do take the leap of faith it can be a rewarding and enriching experience.

If you just want a good laugh at other people's lives read on.

It was always my intention to say who we were and to even name our guests, but my wife cringed at the thought and for the first time in 30 years absolutely put her foot down. My publisher also felt it would be inappropriate, even reckless and so all the names and our location have been changed but otherwise every word is how it has happened even if some of it seems barely believable.

CONTENTS

CHAPTER 1
HOW WE CAME TO RUN A BnB

It was never our intention to run a BnB, it had never even crossed our minds. My Mum and Dad had mentioned doing it some years back but beyond that we hadn't considered it, we hadn't even stayed in many so for us it was something completely new and different.

Here is a little bit of background; I am giving you this because you will see that a lot of this book is filled with observations and plenty of critical analysis. You need to have a little bit of an idea about who we are to understand where we are coming from. We all have a habit of accepting the news and what we are told by journalists, politicians, commentators but unless we know their background, the editor and owner's agendas and their own personal views it is difficult to get an unbiased point of view. I always think we need to have a starting point.

My name is Steve and I have been married to Jane for almost 30 years. We are very different characters, but the combination has worked well for both of us. Jane is very steady which has been a good thing as I have a very low boredom threshold and have done a great many things which has probably tried her patience to the limit but to date Jane has never said no or staged a revolt; although she has dug her heels in over time. Although I have taken us down many roads, some more precarious than others, I have always steadied at the edge of the precipice. Being married to a serial entrepreneur whose take on life is, "If I wake up in the morning and I am not looking forward to the day, it's time for a change," must be challenging for anyone.

I was very lucky as a youngster to be given a private

education. I did not come from a wealthy family, but my parents aspired. One grandfather had been a coal miner, the other a carpenter in London theatres. My mother, who was the driving force, counted money at night at Securicor putting it in those little brown envelopes with the clear windows and supplemented her income by driving the other girls there and back, arriving home at five in the morning. She also cleaned wealthy people's houses during the daytime to put me through school. We also had the advantage that in the 1970s, there was a major tax break for companies whose staff educated their children privately which has long since gone. My father worked for an engineering company and was able to take advantage of that.

Even though my school fees were only £40 a term in 1971 it was still a lot of money. Compare that to 2018 where the same fees are now £9,500 a term. I came from a background where money was tight whilst most of my school friends came from affluent professional households, entrepreneurs and old money. It was never a problem, money was rarely discussed, and it never really registered to me that it was anything special that they skied in Lech and holidayed in Tuscany. I was always very happy spending summers on The Isle of Sheppey. In my last term I remember sitting on a grassy knoll during a cricket match chatting to a friend. We only socialised at school, so I didn't really know much about him.

"Frank," I said, "What are you doing when we finish school in a few weeks?"

"What do you mean?" he replied.

"Are you going to University or have you got a job lined up?"

"I have got a house in Eton Square and £3m in my trust fund, I shall spend the summer in St Tropez and then get involved in the family business perhaps".

He is now part of a billionaire dynasty, but it meant nothing to me at the time; that was just how it was.

I was due to go to university but started working in the summer for a friend's father in his timber business which I loved. I had always had an entrepreneurial spirit and made lots of money even whilst at school, buying and selling, setting up a gardening business in the holidays employing friends as the work came in, then a decorating business that paid more. But it was always the buying and selling that really appealed. I was lucky enough to acquire a car whilst still at school and ran a little taxi service on the side taking friends home and picking them up. This meant I always had cash in my pocket and I got a taste for it.

It took a few weeks before my parents realised I hadn't gone to university as planned. I had been staying at a friend's, but they were understanding. The other important thing was that I couldn't stand being in an office. I always enjoyed being outdoors and being physically energetic. I also had working class roots that weren't going to shift in one generation.

A couple of years went by and I worked my way up but realised there was no future for me working in a family business and as I was only interested in getting to the top, I left and started my own timber business. With no capital it was always a struggle and after another couple of years my mother told me I had to get on and do something else, so we started an auction house together in Bermondsey. In the early 1980s, Bermondsey was a very different place to the one we know today, rough around the edges would be generous, London was a very different city back then.

Bermondsey was the centre of the antiques trade, so it made a lot of sense having an auction house there, but we were naïve and, although it was great fun it was never going to make a fortune. In the days when you could just start up and have a go without lots of compliance and certificates it was great fun. I became the auctioneer and built a modest reputation being employed by Iranian rug dealers to sell their hand-made carpets in Aberdeen to oil workers. Crazy times!

I rented the premises next door to the auction rooms to sell a bit of timber on the side. It was the right place and right time. I was the first lorry onto the old docklands to deliver the timber that pegged out what we now know today as Canary Wharf. For the next two years my little business grew exponentially as we delivered timber to all the Docklands developments that you can see today lining the Thames and beyond.

It was at this time that Jane and I met at a Madonna concert. A minibus of ten girls had booked to go to Wembley in August 1987 but one had to drop out. Thinking those odds were very good I jumped in and eighteen months later we were married on a beach in St Lucia.

Bored of the wood yard I sold it off and went into property development during the boom of the late 1980s only to come a cropper as interest rates rose to 15% and owing the banks a lot of money. We rented out the properties we had and moved to rural Staffordshire whilst the market recovered.

We knew a friend of a friend who was renting a small country estate and whilst visiting they showed us around. We loved the Gardeners Cottage with walled garden and moved there almost immediately. Within a couple of months, I had become the estate Bailiff and raised the rental income by 500%. That was more to do with it being a shambles rather than my management skills.

Looking for a new venture I joined a company to set up a chain of builders' merchants but found it tedious. One day whilst gardening I decided I wanted a nice water barrel. Unfortunately, I couldn't just buy one but found three hundred in a distillery in Ireland. That was the start of our gardening business that started off manufacturing planters, water features and so on and morphed into importing pottery, furniture and opening a garden centre. During this time, we also had our two children and moved home to the most amazing Elizabethan Manor house with workshops and an eccentric landlady.

Waking one morning to find myself bored of the manufacturing I found a buyer for it and concentrated on the garden centre which was good fun for a while. By 1999 the tediousness of a seven day week was getting too much. With a couple of friends, we looked at jumping on the back of the technology boom. We entered The Sunday Times and 3i Technology Catapult competition along with 5000 others from across Europe and won £2m of funding to start a technology business.

As you can guess, by now I was bored with the garden centre which became history for us and so I concentrated on the new internet business. Sadly, like so many others at the time it didn't work out although I left with a part of the business that I developed over the next few years into a very successful sourcing and importing business. Around about this time we bought Marlow House which was to become the house where our children grew up. It was a fantastic family home in a slightly elevated position with wonderful neighbours; we were very lucky.

For the next few years I travelled extensively to the Far East sourcing and organising the manufacture of all sorts of gardening products. I had a great business partner and we had a hoot. I clearly remember Jane asking me in about 2007 when I would get bored and want a change and I replied that it wouldn't happen this time that I would carry on as it was a lot of fun and brought stability to the family. In 2008 the financial crisis came, and our lovely bankers HSBC truly shafted us. I was called into their office and told that our facilities were being reduced by 70% and our interest rate was almost doubling. I asked when this was happening and was told, "from today". I immediately went to see our accountants who told me that couldn't happen. Over the next few months it happened to almost every small business. It just so happened that we were the first in Staffordshire. I asked our bank manager to give me three months to sort everything out. During that time they stopped factoring our debts, at one point sending an email that read, "we no longer have an appetite for business in Ireland". It was the worst possible time in our trading cycle, but I nevertheless managed to trade out and sold the business upstream to our suppliers for a pittance. The whole business was taken away from us as the banks all headed for the doors. *Que sera.* I have never trusted a bank since.

Ten months later the same bank manager telephoned me. I was in Bristol at The Banksy Exhibition. She told me that we had done such a great job of sorting out our finances that the bank wanted to do a case study on us and would that be OK. The other visitors around me were much more surprised by what they then heard rather than the artworks they were seeing.

I quickly had to find something else to do as Jane was giving me that look that I had experienced a few times before. At a dinner party with friends everyone was talking about the financial crash and everyone had an opinion on it. Having always been interested in Economics I went home and wrote down a few of my thoughts. Thinking it read rather well I Googled UK's most successful Hedge Fund Manager who also liked what I had written and invited me to see him. We struck up a collaboration that lasted for the next six years and was the most enjoyable work I have ever done, being paid handsome Mayfair wages to research, think, and write what I liked, when I liked. It was a time of privilege and when I look back on some of the work I produced it was incredibly prescient. I wrote in 2012 about the fallacy of University education for all and the funding issues and long-term problems it would cause young people who built up debt, which is the topic of the day in 2018.

Because of the nature of the work at the Hedge Fund I also found the time to teach sport part time at my local school, these were halcyon days. One problem that did occur though was that I found myself getting quite lonely working from home all the time. I used to go to the offices in Mayfair for group meetings which should have been intellectually stimulating but apart from the owner and the chairman who were both delightful I found most of the employees to have enormous chips on their shoulders. They were incredibly dismissive and many of them proved to be small-minded and surprisingly narrow in their thinking given their educations. People often talk about the Westminster bubble and the London journalists who never get out and about. It's much the same for a large swathe of the financial industry who, despite their "factory visits" and time spent with the Financial Directors of their investments, don't really understand the nuts and bolts of how businesses work.

Somehow, I managed to persuade Jane to leave our lovely home at Marlow House and rent a Georgian townhouse in the town centre so that I could work in cafes and public places to be around people. It also worked well because although our daughter had left home our son was at school there, so it meant he could cycle to school which, given the crazy hours they did, worked very well. We had three fantastic years there. One day we were going on holiday and were at the departure gate when I received a phone call from our long-term tenant at Marlow House to tell us his business was going bankrupt and he was leaving. Sometimes things just happen unexpectedly. Marlow is not the sort of house that can be left empty, so we instructed agents to find a new tenant, but we knew we had been very lucky with the previous ones and after a few months of the house being empty we resigned ourselves to moving back in. This coincided with our son finishing at school and very sadly my role with the Hedge Fund ending.

We were at another crossroads and some decisions had to be made. We thought that we might sell Marlow, so we embarked on a refurbishment project for three months and then invited agents in to value the house. We then found that in the wake of the financial crash, with the property market completely flat coupled with the fact that nobody can do DIY anymore and nobody wants to be more than 50 metres from a Costa coffee, there weren't buyers lining up interested in a big house in the country.

I knew that I didn't want to go and get a job. I have always considered myself to be extremely unemployable. I may have had many businesses over the years and employed a lot of people, but I know that I can't do meetings, am not very keen on commuting and don't want to listen to people who love the sound of their own voice but can't decide or come up with an original idea. I considered starting yet another new business but with my utter contempt for banks knew that was probably unrealistic.

When we had been living in town we had foreign language students to stay with us, we thought it would be interesting for our son to meet lots of different people as his school was also in a little bit of a bubble. This had worked very well for us and along with friends who had recently set up a BnB we were inspired. We decided that rather than rattling around wondering what to do we would open as a Bed and Breakfast. It wasn't a huge leap of faith as we had always entertained, we welcomed friends and family and were used to having lots of people around. We were both able to cook, felt we were pretty good with people and so it seemed like a good idea. Because every bedroom already had an *en suite* and a recent loft conversion was up to date with current legislation, there wasn't too much to do to comply and get up and running. We took our first guest in February 2013 and haven't looked back since. A great website and linking to Booking.com and other third-party agents quickly brought a steady flow of guests and before we knew it we were up and away and fully-fledged BnB owners.

I have told my story, but this is a partnership so a little background on Jane. Although I am writing this book much to Jane's chagrin, it is important that you have a bit of a feeling of the sort of person she is.

Jane comes from Essex, one of four children, her father was a pattern maker and mother a cook. She started work for a re-insurance company in the City aged 16. We met when she was 28, four years older than me. As you have probably concluded, she has the patience of a saint and is the calmest and most understanding person you will ever meet. No other woman would have let me chop and change and do whatever I wanted as she did and for that I am eternally grateful. I know I have caused a few scares and we have had some hairy moments as I come up with a new idea almost daily, but we have had a good life together and there has always been food on the table. I talk later about running a BnB with your partner, I can assure you that Jane is the most perfect person to run a BnB with but, sorry to disappoint you, she is already taken.

CHAPTER 2
WHY WOULD ANYONE WANT TO RUN A BnB?

In a recent survey, running a BnB was top of the list of most desirable jobs for happiness; knocking hairdressers off the top spot. Interestingly, being an author came in at number two which in theory should make me the happiest person alive. Of course, this is very subjective and we all have slightly differing motivations.

I don't quite know how the survey drew this conclusion because the biggest question anyone should ask themselves when considering running a BnB is, "How do I feel about having strangers in my house?" For those that couldn't imagine anything worse, running a BnB certainly wouldn't be in their list of things to make them happy.

It is the single biggest thing and if the answer is, "I don't like people in my house," then you really shouldn't be spending any time thinking about it because no matter how cleverly you divide up your premises, how carefully you manage the guests, there will always be a time when you feel that your visitors are in your space. It's the nature of the job. If that is the case skip through to Chapter 9 and enjoy all the stories about our guests.

I would hazard a guess that this immediately discounts half the population. I should also stress that it is no good running the numbers in order to convince yourself that the idea of being self-employed, running your own business and being in control of your own destiny are enough to overcome the negativity of having strangers in your home. There will come a time when it just grates on you and you realise you don't want to do it anymore.

If after much consideration you decide that you are happy to have people you have never met, have no idea what they are like and are prepared to accept them warts and all, then you can start to ask yourself all of the other questions which will determine if you are the right sort of person to run a BnB and critically the sort of person who can make a BnB work.

This is not an industry that will make you rich. It can give you a great lifestyle, but it will never bring you huge financial rewards if that is your thing. The business model for BnBs is extremely simple. It is much the same as hotels.

Room rate x occupation levels - running costs = profit or loss

If you have three rooms that you are going to use for your BnB @ £100 a night, you know that you can earn £300 x 365 = £109,500 as an absolute maximum. Depending on your location and how often you want to be working it is an industry average to work on 70% occupation bringing your gross income down to a little less than £77,000 which is very good from a VAT perspective which I will come to later. Now strip out your breakfast costs, heating, linen and cleaning and you will probably end up with a figure of about £40,000 before refurbishment and maintenance because on this proposed model you are talking about having the equivalent of 1500 people through the house to stay in any given year. That's a lot of wear and tear on carpets, walls, doors, showers and so forth.

On the upside it is a very tax efficient business with most of the running costs of your home coming out of your takings before tax and of course you do get to work from home, won't need to commute and sit on the M25 anymore and certainly won't need to sit in any more pointless meetings listening to Terry from compliance drone on and on.

The only way you can make any significant money from the BnB business is to open a few of them and employ staff. At this point you have become a hotel operator with all the pressures and stresses that you probably hoped to get away from by opening a BnB which will inevitably involve commuting, meetings and listening to Terry from compliance drone on and on. So if its big profits you are after, look elsewhere.

Assuming you have run the numbers and think it might work for you, you need to consider the following issues.

Are you planning to run this on your own or with a partner? Our guests always say to us, "It must be a lot of work running a BnB". They say this almost as a statement rather than a question. The honest answer is that it has its moments but overall, it can afford you a lot of time off if you structure it properly. Clearly the more you subcontract things like the laundry, cleaning, gardening, maintenance, then the lower your earnings. It is a lot of work for one person and if it isn't going particularly well and it becomes a struggle to get bookings then it could be overwhelming because the tendency would be to try and make every enquiry happen which might not leave anytime to have a break. It is very easy to fall into the trap of trying to take every booking enquiry that comes your way.

It is a business that works well as a partnership. The most successful partnerships are husband and wife or couples who have been together a long time. If the two partners have been together a long time but have pursued different careers or basically have spent the days apart for whatever reasons it may be a leap of faith to believe they can work harmoniously together running a BnB. There are roles and responsibilities, so the question is whether both partners can take direction and possibly work subserviently in some situations. There must be a lot of give and take, plenty of understanding and critically the workload needs to be split in a way that is deemed equitable. That doesn't mean to say the roles and responsibilities are split 50/50, everything in life is about perspective. Both partners need to feel that their partner is pulling their weight and not shirking.

If you have reached the point where you feel you can accept strangers in your home, happy to take a potential reduction in income for a different lifestyle, feel you can either work very hard on your own or can get on very well with your partner then you are at the point to start considering the more practical matters.

Do you have the right property to run a BnB or are you considering buying a property from which to run one? Clearly, you will need to run the maths as you would do with any new business venture. I have already explained the very simple financial formula to running a BnB, you will need to work out any financing costs to acquire a BnB already running, or a property that could make a BnB. Make an allowance for upgrades, permissions and marketing and enter that into your formula under "Costs of doing business" Many of these will be fixed: mortgage, council tax whilst many more will be variable: sausages, bacon, gas and electric.

A few years ago, you would have had to pay careful attention to marketing. You still do but it is no way as complicated as it used to be, but it comes with a cost and a sting in the tail.

Today there are a whole host of third party agents looking to take a slice out of your turnover and make an enormous dent in your profits by helping to drive business to your BnB. The good news is that if you are starting from nothing these are very effective ways of getting people through your doors. Booking.com, Expedia, Laterooms, Hotels.com and many others use their very advanced analytics to understand customer behaviour whilst their search engine criteria drill down their needs to help populate your rooms. This of course comes at a cost usually between 15% and 23%. These sites obviate the need to build your own website to get started but I would recommend that you do have your own website as quickly as possible. Make sure that potential customers can book through your website too, there are many tools available to enable that. Have a good look around other websites to get a feel for the style that you like, it is important that your website reflects what you are trying to do.

You can also put yourself on the map by running a promotion with one of the many discount promoters like Groupon, Wowcher, and Secret Escapes. Just bear in mind that this will still come up in search engines for many months or years afterwards and may be a hindrance if you try and move more upmarket.

The third option is to register with established websites who are looking for new properties to list. These tend to be exclusive companies with their own customer base such as Alistair Sawdays, and Wolseley Lodges but these companies are coming under increasing pressure from the online travel agents (OTAs,) whose fantastic software and interfaces make booking rooms a very transparent operation for anyone looking to do so.

Running a BnB is also a very strange business in the modern world in that it doesn't suffer the unrelenting scrutiny and compliance that many other businesses do. Of course, your premises will have to comply with all the up to date regulations for health and safety, you will need a fire inspection, PAT testing for your electrical products and you will need to go on a food hygiene course. However, compared to most other business, the compliance is relatively light; especially if you remain three rooms or less.

One of the downsides of the BnB business is the fact that your busiest times are generally the weekends. If your friends are still engaged in the daily grind of 9-5, five days a week then most of your social events will still by default be on a Friday or Saturday evening. This shouldn't be a problem as the evenings tend to be quiet in a BnB once you have overcome the whole checking in of guests which I will come to later. However, it is a brave man or woman who would entertain preparing breakfast for guests with a monumental hangover. As you spend more time running your BnB though you really learn to appreciate going out in the week when everything is quieter and cheaper.

So, what are the real upsides of running a BnB? There really are so many that you can understand why that survey said that BnB owners were some of the happiest people.

Depending on your financial situation you can choose to work when you want. Of course, some guests book a long way in advance, but you may choose to only take bookings up to 8 weeks at a time. You may choose not to work at all on a Monday, Tuesday, and Wednesday bearing in mind that guests will have checked out by 11am on the Sunday and wouldn't arrive until after 3pm on a Thursday, almost five days off. You can also block out any dates if there is an event or if you want to go away on holiday. You may also consider extending your availability by finding someone local to run things in your absence, as we do, and it works very well for us and those that help us. If you have always been a workaholic and you think that running a BnB will help you to get over this affliction you will need to be very disciplined because there is the very real danger of working constantly whilst running a BnB. It can very easily be a 7 days a week business. You may decide to offer evening meals which really does ramp up the workload. With the right approach, starting point and discipline you can make the BnB work for you; if you don't have the discipline you will quickly find yourself working for the BnB. As you go along you will find all kinds of short cuts and time saving methods, but you must be open to them.

By delegating and splitting the roles you can create more leisure time, but you must be strict about the roles otherwise you will find yourselves constantly crossing over. In our BnB, Jane looks after housekeeping, shopping, and accounts. I manage breakfasts, marketing, and maintenance. We have some cross over in dealing with guest enquiries but otherwise we tend to stick quite strictly to our roles. This means that if I always do breakfasts then Jane knows that she can go to Pilates or classes at the gym. Equally by leaving all housekeeping to Jane I know that as soon as I have finished breakfast the rest of the day is my own although there are times of the year when we do a lot of maintenance.

Another brilliant upside is meeting lots of great people. As you will see, I have written in this book about some difficult guests but in the great scheme of things this really is a minority. Most of our guests are lovely. We have met some interesting people who have become friends as they have returned on numerous occasions over the years. One guest in particular, gave me such great advice over a business proposition that it made me change my whole life around for the better. Overall most people who have come to stay with us have genuinely wanted to be here and have therefore arrived with the intention of having a good time. Consider how many jobs there are where the customer doesn't really want to be there. This is one of the reasons why hairdressers have always been some of the happiest people because their customers are generally pleased to be there and are usually even happier when they leave. It's the same with running a BnB. Let's face it, this might explain why suicide rates are highest amongst doctors and dentists, there aren't many of their patients who want to be there.

When we were setting up for the BnB we were naturally talking to everyone we could to gather information. We arranged for Staffordshire Tourism to come and see us so that we could get our star rating which, at the time we thought was critical. We spoke to people about food hygiene, health and safety, other businesses about marketing and so on. In hindsight we made some mistakes but not so many that it caused a problem. But here I would like to tell you some of those which are easily avoidable.

CHAPTER 3
EVENING MEALS

The first is about evening meals. We had a lovely lady come to see us from the tourist office who had herself run a BnB in the past. We talked about many aspects of the business and the subject of catering and the meals we would serve obviously cropped up. Naturally we were planning to serve breakfasts because after all, we are called "Marlow House Bed & Breakfast" although I am not sure that counts for much as it seems very rare to be offered a breakfast at any of the AirBnB properties, perhaps they should rename themselves AirB.

The lovely lady then asked us if we were going to serve evening meals. We had already discussed this together because we love cooking and we said that we would. She then explained that we should be very wary as it may not always be profitable. Our view was that we were running the house anyway and with food margins around 400% it would be worth our while. It is only in hindsight that we realised she was correct.

There is the potential for profit from food but as a rule of thumb it comes in two ways:

Top end restaurants charging huge amounts of money for little amounts of food and extraordinary prices for drinks or restaurants that can pack very large numbers of diners in and get significant economies of scale.

The headline profit of 400% looks so appealing but it is the labour cost that makes it so challenging. It is a very similar amount of work to cook for 20 people as it is for 2. Let me explain.

We always asked our BnB guests in advance if they would like to eat here. This meant that we had virtually no food waste; you tend not to anyway when you run a BnB as you can generally use up any spare yourselves which would help to maximise any potential profit.

When guests booked, we would ask them if they would like to eat here one evening. Once one couple said they would like to eat and we knew we would be cooking, we would then ask all the other guests. We had a very nice menu, all freshly prepared and we aimed for good quality, interesting dishes trying to differentiate ourselves from local gastropubs. We found that some evenings we might only be cooking for two guests, on other occasions for eight guests. On some occasions we might be cooking for a pre-bridal wedding party of 14. The workload was quite similar.

Firstly, once the menus were agreed we would have to go shopping. We would tie this in with other shopping or trips to town, so it wasn't too onerous but nevertheless it had to be done and would take upwards of two hours. Once at the shops, it took the same amount of time to shop for two, eight or fourteen people.

We would start laying the table mid-afternoon about four o'clock. There is more work to lay for fourteen than there is for two but not much more. The table still needs a tablecloth (that requires washing afterwards) and because we always dress our table nicely and use candles and decorations on the table, the costs are the same for two or fourteen diners. Then we will start preparing. If you have never been in the restaurant trade and your experience is only ever at the dining side of the equation, then it can be quite hard to understand exactly how much work goes into preparing good quality food. The value of the food that you see on your plate will be 20-25% of the value of your bill but the real costs are the time spent bringing that meal to you.

We will generally spend two hours preparing a dinner. Our guests might then come down to the guest lounge at 7pm and enjoy a few *canapés* before sitting down to dinner at 7.30. If it is a bigger group, it is quite likely that some of the group come down a little late and therefore do not sit down to dinner until 7.45 or 8pm. We then continue cooking and serve three courses which will take us to 9.00 - 9.30. Guests may then choose to have coffee and sit and enjoy each other's company until 10 or 11pm and of course, why shouldn't they.

Sometimes guests are having so much fun that we go to bed and leave them enjoying themselves which means we must finish clearing up in the morning. If we have two guests having dinner paying £35 each we can bank £70 with two of us working from 4pm until 10 pm or later. That is twelve hours work between us. Allow £18 to buy all the food and we are left with £52 or £4.30 per hour each and that's not including doing the shopping.

If we have eight guests, we will work exactly the same period of time making £208 or £17 per hour still not including the time spent shopping. This is worthwhile but the problem that a BnB owner has is that once we are committed to cooking for two guests, we don't know how many more we will get to eat that evening.

To compound the problem, most restaurants now offer deals constantly as well as a wide choice on their menu, much wider than we could offer so the number of people who are prepared to pay £35 for a private dining experience in a lovely venue isn't that high.

It is a very difficult situation. We spent two years convincing ourselves that it was worth doing. In fact, our best month we cooked over one hundred dinners, but we were absolutely exhausted with so many late nights, staying up, looking after guests and being considerate and patient hosts and found that all the extra turnover didn't really turn into that much extra profit. A couple of big dinners were great, but we did so many dinners for two where in reality we were losing money.

We do not cook very often for guests anymore, only if it is a group coming together or a special event, usually for a minimum of eight guests. We have groups who regularly return specifically to dine together in a unique environment who also like our style of cooking and presentation but apart from that it is very rare. Guests are often disappointed that we do not offer to cook every night and understandably so, but it really doesn't pay and is very tiring.

We are now so much more appreciative of all the hard work that goes into running a restaurant. We will always leave a very generous tip if the service and the food was good and we will always send a message of thanks to the kitchen. There is nothing more disheartening as a chef when you feel you have prepared something quite special for guests and they barely acknowledge the effort that you have put in. I completely understand that this is the way society has evolved, that we all feel entitled and if we are paying for it then there is no need to show any appreciation but if everyone was to work in a kitchen or front of house for a while and saw the amount of very hard work that goes into presenting a quality meal then they would surely be much more appreciative.

The meal deals that have appeared everywhere can only work financially for the restaurants if they can really fill their covers. It takes a lot of care, attention, and time to produce a well thought out menu and I don’t think that most people appreciate what is involved. From a purely BnB perspective I would suggest from our own experience that catering for evening meals isn't a profitable thing to do unless you can cater for larger groups. However, one of the most profitable businesses in hospitality you could run is a small hotel of 10-12 rooms with a very high-end restaurant within it. There are enough numbers of affluent people and those that work very hard and want to have the occasional special treat who will pay a lot of money to go away for a night and stay in a lovely friendly and intimate hotel with a restaurant that has had great reviews. This wouldn't be the owners necessarily being in the kitchen but

a separately employed professional chef with his or her own staff. Forty or fifty covers at £75 per person is a much more compelling financial proposition especially if many of them stay overnight as well.

CHAPTER 4
WHO VISITS A BnB IN THE STAFFORDSHIRE COUNTRYSIDE?

People are far more sincere and good-humoured at speeding their parting guests than on meeting them – Anton Chekhov

Here at our BnB we get a pretty wide spread of visitors of different ages, social groups, ethnicity. It is by no means truly representative, we aren't cheap, and I am sure there are a lot of people who rarely get the opportunity to visit hotels and BnBs. We are always asked what sort of people come to stay with us here in the Staffordshire countryside, it doesn't seem an obvious destination and, yet we are always busy. In response I always ask, "Have you ever been in a motorway service station on a Sunday afternoon?" It is a fascinating place to be, there are so many different groups of people doing a multitude of things in so many different places. We are so lucky here in the UK. That we can move about freely with good transport links and many of the population are wealthy enough and have plenty of leisure time. Here at Marlow House we get people visiting family, christenings, deaths and plenty of marriages. We have two wedding venues very local which give us a steady stream of visitors. We have walkers enjoying the Staffordshire countryside, historians visiting our wealth of historic buildings, business travellers, motorcyclists and car enthusiasts enjoying the amazing driving close by. Cyclists, sportspeople; a whole plethora of visitors.

Here follow some sweeping generalisations. Of course there are exceptions but not that many:

We have had visitors from Ireland, France, Belgium, Holland, Germany, Switzerland, France, Portugal, Russia, China, Japan, Australia, New Zealand, USA, Canada, Chile and Argentina. Residents from every corner of the UK have been to stay. It never ceases to amaze us how all these different nationalities find a little BnB in the heart of the Staffordshire countryside. That truly is one of the amazing upsides of the internet and the OTAs and review sites. They all are searchable, and the algorithms of Google and others lead searchers to us based on what other visitors have said, it is the ultimate recommendation by word of mouth.

Around 25% of our visitors attend weddings locally. This gives us the biggest spread of the type of guests we see in terms of social groups. The ages vary wildly from babies to grandparents. Some of those guests that stay with us probably wouldn't choose a place like Marlow House in other circumstances. 5% of our visitors come from overseas, 50% of our guests are retirees, the majority of whom are retired public sector workers and the remaining 20% of our guests come for a specific purpose like visiting families or rallying at the local hill climb. We always enjoy having those guests as they invariably fill our drive with their classic cars or racing cars.

As already said, we have had over 3500 people stay since we started the BnB five years ago. This has given us the opportunity to meet so many different sorts of people. We cannot but help to examine our guests like anthropologists and pigeon hole them. We probably shouldn't but it's just human nature. It's not malicious, it's just a reward of the job and we usually do this in a good-hearted way. What we have found though is that there are some extraordinarily constant traits running through different groups.

In the UK, the friendliest and easiest people to have stay are from South Wales and Mid Wales. They are always very jolly and positive. They put family and enjoying life at the centre of everything, are always very complimentary and very chatty. Here at Marlow we dine *en famille* at one large table. This has its advantages and disadvantages. When our guests get on together it can create a lively atmosphere and a real buzz. If guests prefer their own company it can sometimes be a little painful. We always love welcoming someone from South Wales because they will talk to everyone, being very open and very friendly and usually get the breakfast table full of conversation.

Visitors from the South West are also very friendly and share many of the qualities of those from South Wales. Why should this be? We don't know for sure, but I think it comes down to the fact that they accept life and aren't always chasing something, they rarely mention money or what they have and they invariably take life as it comes.

Guests from Liverpool are always good value, often loud, full of laughter and good fun. We always have to laugh because until recently most of our guests from Liverpool would insist on paying us in cash as soon as they arrived whereas most other guests pay us when they leave. Over the last year, people paying in cash has all but disappeared as everyone moves over to paying by card, so this doesn't really happen anymore.

Guests from the Black Country are always very polite and often act as though they shouldn't really be here. I think many of those guests find Marlow House a little daunting even though we try to make it as friendly and relaxed as possible. Black Country guests will always have a full English with black pudding, you would bet the house on it.

Visitors from Manchester are generally OK, but some can be a bit edgy, and given half the chance they will party hard, nothing wrong with that. They tend to be a bit flashier with their cars and clothes. The girls from Liverpool are very relaxed and will spend two days walking round with their rollers in their hair, girls from Manchester would never do that and always have to look ready for a big night out.

Visitors from the North West are generally fine, many of them are lovely but sometimes we can find a few to be a bit difficult but not as challenging as those from Yorkshire and the North East. That isn't fair. Those from Tyneside, Middlesbrough and Newcastle upon Tyne are generally fine but for some reason those from Yorkshire especially North Yorkshire we always struggle with. As I opened with, these are sweeping generalisations and there are always exceptions, and so I hope that any Yorkshire residents don't take offence with these remarks, I am just telling it as we see it. The people from Yorkshire we have had to stay are extremely cautious with their money, will always look for a deal, really aren't very friendly and will try to pick fault in anything. If I had to sum it up I would just say that they weren't very happy. Those from West Yorkshire seem to bear a large chip on their shoulder about things and always let us know how much they have, it really is quite extraordinary.

We have had some lovely guests from the East Midlands, bizarrely we have had a few guests come to stay from Leicester to visit our local Indian restaurant which has been building an extraordinary reputation. We have had many guests from The Fens which seems like a long way to come for a BnB.

Guests from London and the South East are easily the most demanding. Clearly living in a metropolis with such enormous choice has really influenced those residing there. To put this into context, Jane and I both come from the South East, both of our children currently live in North London and our families live in London and Essex. We have many friends who live in London that we regularly visit, and we even have a Christmas Lighting business that we run in London every November for four weeks. Despite all this regular interaction with people from the South east we are still constantly astonished by the attitudes of those visiting us from there.

Almost all our guests are happy to enjoy our breakfasts and overall most people will finish their food. They have very few special dietary requirements. Those from the North West are what we would call salad dodgers, reluctant to have tomatoes and mushrooms but generally most guests will eat most things. There seem to be surprisingly few allergies or eating restrictions. One would imagine that dietary restrictions would be about medical conditions or occasionally moral choices; we have been getting an increasing number of vegetarians from Manchester.

I would now like to dispel the notion, from a BnB point of view, that dietary issues have anything to do with health and well-being but appear to be almost entirely geographic. In fact, almost all our special requests generally are from guests travelling from London and the South East. Whether its gluten, vegan, vegetarian, issues with dairy, they all seem to emanate from the South East. I wonder why that would be?

Guests from the South East seem to have a predilection for making everything a little more difficult than it needs to be. Guests coming up on a Friday for a weekend seem to have no concept of the relationship between distance and time. We always ask what time they think they might arrive. Once we have been told that, we ask what time they are leaving. Despite all the information available online there is very little correlation between the two. In fairness, the M1 and M6 on a Friday afternoon and evening is a lottery but even so, the number of times guests have arrived from the South East at 10 or 11pm is quite extraordinary. Those guests then rarely come down in time for breakfast. It seems that although most Londoners accept that it can take one to two hours to reach the M25 from central London in the early evening, they then believe that the space time continuum alters and that the rest of the UK is only 20 minutes further on. This hasn't happened just once but on many occasions. There is that old joke that Londoners don't know what is north of the Watford Gap, apart from Manchester United supporters, and it is true.

What Londoners consider to be important is often very different to the rest of our guests. It is quite extraordinary how quickly people from the South East can get around to talking about the price of property. This is a topic that is rarely, if ever, brought up by our other guests. The conversation with guests from the South East will take two forms. Either, they haven't been able to get on the property ladder and complain bitterly about how expensive it is. These tend to be the younger Londoners who are eager to bring it up but won't force it. The older guests who are property owners will shoe horn it into the conversation at almost any opportunity. I have one of my internal sweepstakes as to how long it is before they manage to mention it to a table full of guests. It is usually in the context of how hard it is for younger people but will ultimately lead on to how lucky they have been. I love it when we have guests from South Wales who seem to have worked out what life is about and the older Londoners who genuinely believe that you are measured by your wealth.

Guests from the South East also seem to have a disproportionate number of vitamins and tablets. I have no idea why this should be the case, but we see it at first hand. It really is quite surprising, sometimes we believe we can hear them rattle.

We have had guests visit us from Scotland who vary between the very friendly from Glasgow and Edinburgh to quite reserved and quiet the further north they're from.

All our guests from Ireland both North and South have been lovely. The Northern Irish aren't the most organised and tend to be rushing for flights and ferries, those from the South are so super relaxed they wouldn't worry if they missed their plane or ferry altogether, they are just enjoying the *craic.*

Our other guests from around the world have all tended to be lovely. Clearly, they are already quite open-minded; by the fact that they would travel and end up in Staffordshire. But notwithstanding that, we have found them to be interesting and generally extremely polite.

Guests from Europe are always very lovely. Germans can be a little quiet and are generally quite bemused by our English customs. Danes, Dutch and those from Belgium are all always great value and really enjoy our scenery as they tend to have quite flat landscapes.

We have had only four Russians to stay. They came as one group and they were great fun. Only one of them could speak a bit of English but between that, my A Level Russian and plenty of Champagne that they had brought with them we had a great evening; they were very generous.

Some of our loveliest guests have come from Argentina and surprisingly we have had quite a few. They are so passionate about their country, their politics and their culture, we have always found them hugely entertaining. We love guests who really want to engage and share their experiences, it's all part of travelling and one of the things that makes this such a good job.

We have had quite a lot of Americans, in fact last year we had twenty-four Americans visit us. I will talk more about them in the next chapter called Trump and Brexit because their input is fascinating. The press always tends to lampoon the Americans as insular, parochial, and fat. The Americans who stayed with us were certainly not insular or parochial.

Our Japanese guests have been a little painful; the cultural differences are quite significant. They are always extremely polite but generally do not speak English. We can hardly complain, our Japanese has lots of room for improvement.

We have only had two Chinese people stay with us, a mother and daughter whom I will write about in "Guest

Stories". Suffice to say our cultures are poles apart. I spent quite a lot of time in China on business in the noughties and saw first-hand the cultural divide.

Antipodeans are regular visitors to Marlow House. We have had many Australians and New Zealanders stay over the years. New Zealanders can be quite reserved, but they are full of pluck, bearing in mind how remote New Zealand is it is amazing how far they travel. We have one couple who visit Europe for two months every year; impressive!

We do find that Antipodeans have some unusual requests. Quite a few prefer sheets and blankets to duvets. Fortunately, we do have some blankets so not a difficult request, but it does make us realise how much easier it is for housekeeping to use duvets. Large hotels save so much time using duvets instead of sheets and blankets. We also find that they want breakfast at unearthly hours. We always assumed it was because of jet lag and the time difference but they are just used to getting up early, getting work out of the way by 2 o'clock and enjoying the rest of the day. Hard to disagree with that, it does make me wonder why we don't do that here as a society? The schools start and finish earlier in Europe. Why do we feel the need to stay at work until 6pm and beyond? We know that the UK is behind on productivity, I wonder what would happen if we all started work and school at 7am, finished at 2pm and had all that extra leisure time. Would we all be happier and become more productive? Would we have happier family lives if parents could spend all that extra time with their children? Of course, it will not happen as it would undoubtedly be a health and safety issue for everyone going to work and school in the dark, like it is in Norway, Sweden, and Iceland where 32% of the population get knocked over in the dark every fortnight.

When I said that they wanted breakfast at unearthly hours, it isn't really that bad, it's just that we aren't used to getting up that early, I would happily start earlier, and finish earlier given the choice.

Australians aren't that keen on change and tend to order the same breakfasts that they would have at home and sometimes even bring their own cereals with them. We have had some very engaging and delightful Antipodeans stay with us, it is always interesting to hear about other cultures and places from around the world; especially their politics.

CHAPTER 5
PRESIDENT TRUMP AND BREXIT.

If ever there were two subjects that dominated the breakfast table conversations these were them. It really was quite extraordinary over the last twelve months to hear the diametrically opposed opinions around the table, there were times we thought it might come to fisticuffs. Such was the interest and polarisation that even our Yorkshire guests stopped complaining and Londoners momentarily forgot about their housing and weird diets.

If the pollsters had really wanted to know what was going on they should have just asked BnB owners. We knew what was going to happen just from the many conversations we heard every morning. Of course, we didn't have the entire populations of the UK and the USA here, but it did give us an extraordinary insight that wasn't really portrayed in the many TV debates and newspaper discussions.

What we did see was that those controlling the media were singing off a very different hymn sheet to the general population. Everyone has since found this out in hindsight, but we saw it at first hand throughout 2016 and early 2017.

I should stress once again that we do not see all sections of society here at Marlow House by any stretch of the imagination. As most of our guests come from the large swathe of Middle England we rarely see those struggling to get by which, we appreciate, is a very sizeable cohort. We also tend to have a higher proportion of older people rather than younger which will also skew things. However, we do get a lot of retired public sector workers whom I would have thought would vote to remain; why upset the status quo when you are on to a good thing?

In the run up to the referendum the breakfasts at Marlow House were looking more like 'Question Time'. Some guests were keen to discuss everything and would embark on a discussion before they had even sat down, others showed no interest but were cajoled into it. If there was a particularly quiet table with a chilly air I would throw a small pebble into the pond of silence by asking how people were planning on voting. An hour later the table could not have been more animated; it was a BnB owners dream. One of our challenges running a BnB is to get guests engaged, it is such a tricky path to tread, some guests are super friendly and want to chat, others are shy, would like to chat but struggle to start. Some prefer to enjoy their own company but don't really let on. Thank goodness Jane and I spent nine years at the Sigmund Freud University of Human Understanding and Psychology otherwise we would be in a real pickle!

We very quickly found out the differing opinions between those in the major Metropolitan areas and those outside of them. What was very interesting was that the Remainers from the Metropolitan areas had no interest at all in entering a discussion that might have changed their minds, they were right and that was the end of it, everyone else as far as they were concerned were deluded, stupid or racists. Everyone else bar a good-sized minority who had also decided to vote Leave were open to discussion and ideas. What we constantly saw was the intransigence of the Remainers and their inability or reluctance to discuss different perspectives. This attitude seemed to sway those who were undecided. After the referendum during the post-mortem this was a conclusion that the media, reporters, and analysts also came to. We could have told them this a month before the election. It was the same when President Barack Obama came over to the UK and then started telling everyone what they should be doing as though he was the font of all knowledge. He didn't realise that for many people their decision was based upon the nuances of British life, the minutiae of how their lives were affected by the issues being discussed; very few people were interested in any bigger pseudo intellectual argument.

As these conversations evolved in the six months leading up to the referendum the issues that were being discussed changed. Where immigration dominated the early discussions, latterly it was more about taking back control. This was initially from Brussels, but it started to morph into taking back control from Parliament and then London. It really was quite surprising to see that divide which has subsequently been written about at length. Even though we had a pretty good idea how the result would be, it was still a great shock to wake up to it the day after the referendum. The press and pollsters who dominated the airwaves and news agencies just kept telling us we would vote "Remain".

We then experienced another eight months with the Remainers gleefully telling any guests they could find that we were all doomed. It was quite laughable; like living through a tired pantomime.

The day of the referendum results I was serving breakfast to 8 guests, four of whom were from London and had made clear that they were staunch Remainers, the other four were clearly quite ambivalent, I don't know how they voted. As the news was still coming through, it seemed appropriate to have the news on that morning, and there were audible gasps worthy of a Vaudeville production. As the stock market went into free fall the four guests were talking about the end of the UK as we know it. They blamed all the feckless and ignorant people who voted to leave who were causing this utter catastrophe. By the end of breakfast, the markets had recovered and were up on the start of the week, the UK didn't break away from the continental shelf and start drifting towards the Azores and riots didn't break out in Ripon. They sheepishly left but with dire warnings of the future. We are just a humble little Bed and Breakfast in the Staffordshire countryside but even we felt the wrath of the ill-conceived referendum. There is a very good reason we don't have referendums here in the UK, they are divisive and will inevitably split opinions, families, co-workers and even bed and breakfast guests.

Fortunately, as time went on, the drama subsided gently, time heals all wounds, but this seemed quite unnecessary really. Events in Europe are overtaking our little referendum. History may say that we in the UK were a catalyst for change; those fervent pro-European historians may even lay the blame of a fractured Europe at our door. But the referendum was only a symptom of bigger problems at the core of the European Union.

In 2016 we also had 26 American visitors. If we thought the lead up to the referendum took an age, American elections make us look as though we had rushed ours. From as early as January 2016 our American guests were talking about the US nominations. The English press like to portray Americans as very insular suggesting that only 159 people in America own a passport and that's generally to go to Canada for Pop Tarts. For some inexplicable reason as well, there is a huge emphasis on trailer trash, the unemployed black population of decaying Detroit and low paid Mexican workers. Aside from these groups everyone else is either a beautiful Hollywood actress or actor, a Silicon Valley geeky billionaire or is in Congress.

I find it strange to think that our reporting of the US is so polarised given that they are the leading economic power in the world, the leading military power and have been our allies for many years despite the subjugation they suffered prior to the War of Independence.

None of our guests fit the profile sold to us by our media. Overall our American visitors have been delightful, well-travelled, educated, some with their own businesses, university lecturers, some who worked for large corporations, others for smaller concerns. Once again, not a complete spectrum but representative of the middle classes. For some reason the majority of these were historical Republican voters, half men, half women. We had six Democrats stay with us during this time.

In the first half of the year whilst the primaries were happening, they were collectively embarrassed by the name calling and the public washing of dirty laundry. Generally, they felt that Donald Trump was unlikely to win the nomination and they tended to tow the general line fed by the media that he was a joke and just doing it for his own vanity. By May when Donald Trump won the Primary they were generally shocked and embarrassed how this would look to the rest of the world. This continued as the Clinton-Trump debates started.

By the autumn, our American guests were apologising for what they considered to be a complete shambles, however, faced with the choices nearly all of them said that they would vote for Donald Trump. The logic was something we might find difficult to comprehend here in the UK. It was split into two very specific camps.

One group explained that in America when you look in the mirror what you see generally tells you how you vote; if you are a woman, a white man, a black man, blue collar or white collar. It is in your bones and you do not deviate from that. This forms a core of the vote and the politicians know that this group are very unlikely to be moved. Perhaps that has some resonance here in the UK, but recent events have shown that people can be swayed with the right arguments.

The other issue was whom you loathed less. Whilst many of our guests said truthfully or otherwise that they didn't really like Donald Trump although they felt he talked a lot of sense, they couldn't bear to vote for Hilary Clinton whom they felt they couldn't trust and they were fed up with what they saw as Nepotism. They were positively saying that they would vote for Trump. By the time November came however American guests became very reluctant to say which way they were going to vote. On our relatively small sample it seemed likely that Donald Trump would win but we can certainly understand why the pollsters got it wrong; it all happened on the day, those that hadn't wanted to say, came out and voted for Trump.

The six Democrats we had during the year were adamant in their loathing for Donald Trump so in many respects they weren't the interesting part of the analysis as they were never going to be swayed.

Once again, if pollsters really want to get an idea of what may happen, ask BnB owners, we have our finger on the pulse! Approaching somebody on the street whose guard is up is unlikely to get the most honest answer. Ask someone when they have had a good night's sleep and is enjoying a cooked breakfast looking out over the beautiful Staffordshire countryside and you find they are more relaxed and therefore more likely to tell you as it is.

It is very easy to look on at American politics in disbelief, but we must remember that our starting point is so completely different to that of our American cousins. Here in the UK a budding Prime Minister starts his or her career pounding the streets of a constituency promising Mrs Jones that if she votes the right way he/she will do everything in their power to get the Council to mend her driveway. Assuming they win the by-election and get voted to become a backbencher, they will then have to go through a learning period, towing the line following the Whip until they get spotted after producing lots of papers and questions in the Commons. Theresa May following a career at the Bank of England stood for Parliament in 1992 and 1994 only getting elected in 1997. She then held various roles in the shadow cabinet from 1999-2010. Once the Conservatives got into power in a coalition in 2010 she was able to rise through the ranks becoming Home Secretary but still had to wait until the referendum and the resignation of David Cameron to get the chance to run as party leader and then by default as Prime Minister. She may well have become party leader when the Conservatives were not in power in which case she would have had to defend her seat in Maidenhead and then hope the Conservatives win the election for her to become Prime Minister.

Compare this to the American system which seems much more drawn out and convoluted but is in fact much more direct. With no experience at all but with powerful and rich backers, anyone in theory can run for office. A list of party nominees then battles it out to become top dog whether they are currently serving or complete novices. Once they have won that battle as Donald Trump did as a novice they then battle it out along party lines, in his case taking on Hilary Clinton with decades of Governmental experience. He announced he would run in June 2015 and beat Hilary Clinton in November 2016. So, from start to finish Donald Trump with no previous Governmental experience won the American election in 17 months something that took Theresa May 24 years to achieve. It took David Cameron 9 years, Gordon Brown 24 years, Tony Blair 14 years, Margaret Thatcher 20 years. America is very different, but we always look at it through our own prism because we perceive Americans to be the same as us.

CHAPTER 6
ETIQUETTE

Definition:
"The customary code of polite behaviour in society or among members of a particular profession or group."

Reality:
"Some cause happiness wherever they go; others, whenever they go."
Oscar Wilde

Life is all about equilibrium. The Ying and Yang, finding balance. One of the great misbalances of Planet Earth is the relationship between guests and hotel and BnB owners. As Max Beerbohm the essayist once said, "Mankind is divisible into two great classes: hosts and guests".

It all starts with the booking process. Potential guests can search online or through publications. A BnB must bare its soul, show pictures of all aspects to court the potential guest, always putting on the finest show. To succeed the BnB must always try to provide the highest levels of service, cleanliness and hospitality regardless of what might be thrown at us because in this modern world, poor reviews can have a disproportionate effect on a small business. Prospective bookers can anonymously peruse a multitude of places to stay, picking holes in the photos, the facilities, location, and decor. They will then vote with their credit card and arrive full of expectation. At this point they have made their choice. It may have been the first one they came across, it may have been on a personal recommendation or it may have been the last room available in their geographic requirement. Whatever reason for choosing, the guest has had many opportunities to make the choice of a BnB where they think they will be looked after and made comfortable and they will probably by now have some preconceptions about their hosts.

The BnB owners at this point have no idea who their guests are, what they are like and have no vetting or control in having them to stay. It has never happened to us, but I would imagine it is a pretty rare occurrence that a BnB owner has ever declined entry to any guests upon arrival. In our very liberal world it would probably end up as a court case if they did even though it is our home, we have very few rights in whom we can potentially decline. A constant scam is that some guests threaten owners with terrible reviews unless they waive their room charge. It is very difficult for an owner to get those reviews taken down by the online review companies, such is the balance of power.

So, from the hotelier's perspective there seems to be a lot more Ying than Yang. As you read this book you may get the impression that most guests are challenging or even a nightmare but that just isn't the case. Most of our guests have been lovely but that wouldn't make for interesting reading, so the stories tend to be about the "more interesting ones". They represent a small minority so if you are thinking about running your own BnB don't be swayed by these stories, they make great dinner stories with friends and really help you appreciate the lovely guests who make up the majority. They have certainly made us giggle even if some drive us to distraction.

Life for the hotelier and BnB owner would be much easier if guests were able to appreciate things from the owner's perspective and consider these few examples of hotel etiquette. I don't think these are outrageous or in any way an attempt to curb freedoms and liberties, they are just modern manners. Some of what follows is just common-sense, others are very specific and drive us nuts.

Booking your room

In a very short space of time there has been an extraordinary shift in people's behaviour when it comes to booking. This has been in part driven by_Booking.com and others who actively promote "free cancellation". It has somehow become acceptable for prospective guests to book two or three hotels simultaneously, to "have them in the bank" so that they can choose nearer the time which one suits them best. This is a problem for all hoteliers but not a disaster for a town centre hotel with 50 rooms. If the guest decides to cancel this room a few days before, it is quite possible that a town centre hotel in high demand might be able to sell it to someone else and if they don't it would represent a loss of 2%. If it was with our BnB for example with 4 rooms, cancelling a few days before would almost certainly lead to a loss of 25%.

This may seem perfectly acceptable behaviour especially as Booking.com are actively encouraging you to book anything by telling you that you can cancel but from the owner's point of view it is extremely damaging and quite rude. What will now have to happen is that hotels and BnBs will have to take pre-payments to secure the room and stop late cancellations. It is not even enough to just have the credit card number because the industry is constantly being given false numbers so that when a guest doesn't show, and the hotel tries to take payment for loss of earnings the card is declined. Hotels will have no choice but to take a pre-payment which doesn't really suit anyone. The press is constantly full of stories of patients who don't turn up to their GP appointment costing the rest of the taxpayers money. Generally, everyone agrees that this is unacceptable. I struggle to see the difference between not turning up for the GP appointment, after all the GP has allocated that time and can never get it back, to booking a room and not turning up or cancelling very late, the hotelier can never get that revenue back. How would guests feel if they turned up for work and their employer said that he didn't want them today and wouldn't be paying them?

It is strange the way this has even evolved. If you want to go to a Robbie Williams concert you can't book a ticket to be paid for on the night should you decide that you want to go.

BnB owners always try to be positive and welcoming, but should you arrive one day and they aren't quite as chirpy as you might have expected it could well be that they have had unexpected cancellations that were going to pay for the heating oil or electricity that month. Please don't think that because BnB owners often live in a nice house that they are millionaires and just doing this for the benefit of everyone else. Like most people they have bills to pay and are running a business, albeit a more unusual one but a business none the less. This is a real problem. Two years ago, we had cancellations only due to death, mutilation, or imprisonment, we now get one in four of our online bookings cancelled at some stage or another. It's very painful and given it didn't happen before, quite unnecessary. It has just become part of peoples' psyche and is actively encouraged by the phraseology of the online travel agents.

Information

When booking a room at a BnB it is useful to let the owners know what time you might arrive, if you have any special dietary requirements, if you have children with you and if they might need a travel cot for example. For most people this might seem very logical to let the owners know because it will almost certainly enhance their stay and make life easier for everyone. However, there are some guests who prefer to keep their cards close to their chests. We don't know why this is and it is their prerogative. Part of the problem may be about reading emails.

When our son started working for a bank in London,

one of the first little courses he went on within the bank was about writing an internal email. He and everyone else on that course was told that an email should be no more than two sentences long because that is generally all that anyone will bother to read. When he told us this we thought they were joking but it is very true as we have found out and continue to do so at ours and our guest's cost.

Whenever we reply to a booking there are things we like to ask and tell our guests.

Firstly: "What time will you arrive? Our check in is usually from 3pm and check out by 11am. If you require an earlier check in because you are going to an event, please let us know. If you are travelling late, please let us know."

Hmm. That's already two lines but we do need to know. We are a BnB, it's just that Jane and I don't sit at a reception desk all day waiting for guests to arrive although some guests think we do or at least we ought to.

Secondly: "Please let us know if you have any special dietary requirements." We could say that we have seen you are travelling from London, so we assume you will want the Quinoa Toast with cocoa butter and eggs laid by chickens that do Pilates. We ask this question because vegetarian sausages must be defrosted, and we don't have loaves of Gluten free bread lying around. Pre-warned is pre-armed. We have spotted a direct correlation with the guests with the most specific requests regarding food or allergies and the guests who fail to reply to emails. It's probably just coincidence, they are just very busy managing their own personal challenges.

Thirdly: "Satnavs can have a tremendous sense of humour and some brands will take you on a guided tour of the Staffordshire Countryside. We are within sight of the main trunk road and we recommend that you follow the directions on our website or just follow the Main road for exactly 5 miles from the ring road, then turn left for our village. We are the big house on the left."

It wasn't that many years ago when people would have asked for directions or looked on our website or even gone to Google Maps. That has completely changed, 98% of our visitors only use their satellite navigation devices in their cars, their phones, or their Tom Toms. Whatever these devices tell us now is taken as gospel.

Sadly, our mention of directions is third on the list and never ever gets read. Marlow House is a large Victorian Rectory property with cedar trees in front. It is very imposing which is why we use that image on all our literature and the website including all the online travel agents. Whenever you look us up that is the picture that you see. At the bottom of the drive just in case you don't look up and see the 180-year-old Lebanese Cedars rising in front of a very large imposing white house we have a large piece of sandstone in the wall carved out with the words "Marlow House".

It takes a certain genius not to be able to find us as you can clearly see us from the main trunk road and yet 25-30% of our guests would never consider disputing what the lovely lady who lives in their satnav says even when she starts directing them over hill and dale to the middle of nowhere taking our guests miles out of their way. It is one of those idiosyncrasies of modern life. We have thought about telling the satnav companies but where would you start? Ringing customer services of Hyundai in Seoul in South Korea to explain that Marlow House can be seen from the road? I can imagine how that conversation would go.

What is most annoying is that when our guests are eventually told by the lovely lady who lives in their device that "you have reached your destination" it looks nothing like our house in all the pictures that they have seen. They are invariably at our little hamlet's crossroads or outside one of our lovely neighbour's houses, which are usually charmingly beautiful but little cottages. That doesn't stop them knocking on the door with all their luggage in hand. One couple of guests actually walked straight in with their luggage when the door was opened which has remained a source of much amusement in our little hamlet.

We have recently had discussions as to how any signage might read that our guests might be able to understand and follow. That of course would require them to look up and potentially ignore the very persuasive and reliable lady who has made their satnav her home.

I did have one guest who arrived complaining bitterly that we were very difficult to find and that there were no signs. He was quite obstreperous. I had already checked that I had sent him directions by email and a note to ignore his satnav. He rang me four times during the latter stages of his journey trying to find us. At one stage he was only 60 yards away but still managed to drive for a further five miles before eventually arriving in a foul mood. He said that there were no signs even as he approached the house. I politely said that was most strange and wondered if our signs had been removed. He kindly walked back down the drive with me. As we both looked at the five-foot-wide by 18" high piece of sandstone carved "Marlow House" in the wall next to the gate that he passed as he drove up the drive there was a stony silence. There was an opportunity for a crushing blow but always being too polite and not having been paid yet I asked, "Would you like a nice cup of tea and a piece of cake after your difficult journey?". Nothing more was said.

The fourth thing that we sometimes need to ask on our email is: "If you are attending a wedding or event in the area will you require a taxi? We are quite rural, and they can take a while to come so it is generally prudent to book one in advance".

As you can see, we have four things that we like to ask our guests all of which would help their stay enormously, but we now know that they will only read two lines, so which one goes to the top? The one that means they might find us hidden as we are in the Shire deep in Hobbit country. The one that might mean they get things they can eat? Perhaps the one where they tell us what time they are arriving, so we can be here to let them in or the one that means they have transport to get them to their event. Such a dilemma.

Of course, these have now all been pushed further down the list by the new mail that insists we have a deposit because, so many people are now cancelling "because they can". If anyone, anywhere has any suggestions as to how we can get guests to read our emails please let us know and we will be eternally grateful.

So, guests have booked, they may come, they may not, they may cancel, they may not. They may read things we tell them to make their stay easier and more enjoyable, they may not. Let's assume though that overcoming all these hurdles, including that mad women who lives in their satnav with the crazy sense of humour, they actually arrive at Marlow House, what next?

Here at Marlow we usually say that check in is from 3pm and check out is by 11am. These times aren't completely arbitrary, neither are they cast in stone, but they are suggested for good reason. We appreciate that guests who have events to attend may need to check in earlier. If they are attending a wedding which starts at 2pm it is logical that they want to check in and change at perhaps 12.30. We will always try and accommodate. Equally if they are staying the night before a wedding they may not want to check out until 1.30 to go to the wedding, again we will try and work with them.

As any sane and reasonable person can conclude with guests checking out at 11am there is a period of time required to make up the rooms, change the linen, clean and tidy. We continue in our spare time to try and control the space time continuum and Jane is making enormous progress on developing her "tear in time theory" to allow us to potentially halt time so that we can get the cleaning done faster for our guests but at the present we just aren't there yet. We completely understand that this is an inherent weakness on our part and for this we apologise.

Those guests that arrive at 11am on the dot are often surprised that their room isn't ready. Once again, the positioning of the sentence in our email about arrival times came too late and their attention span did not carry them through to the third line. They are generally quite understanding especially when we sit them down with a cup of tea and a piece of cake. We could of course tell them they are four hours early and to clear off, but we only do that quietly and internally. This is a classic example where the balance of power is skewed. We sadly don't have the opportunity to be ready 4 hours late for our guests. We wouldn't have much of a business if our rooms weren't ready until 7 o'clock in the evening. So, as a matter of etiquette, it is very useful to let the BnB owners know what time you are arriving just so that they can be ready for you.

Some guests understandably must work until the end of the day before they can travel. In these instances, we would also like to be informed. Whilst we appreciate that some guests feel we should be on call 24/7 and the requirement to sleep, rest or have a life might be a considerable inconvenience to their overall enjoyment it is just good manners to let us know if they are going to be late.

Running a BnB isn't like running a hotel. We are a very small business where we are chefs, housekeepers, administrators, marketeers, PR gurus, congenial hosts, gardeners and general builders. We have a certain amount of flexibility, but we still have things that we need to do.

Recently we had a family who rang us to say they would be arriving at 7pm. That's great, very polite, keeping us informed so that we can get on and do other things. They eventually arrived at 10.15. Naturally we thought they had had an accident, got lost, stuck in traffic and obviously their mobile phones had run out of power. It transpired that they thought they would have dinner on the way, made a diversion to a restaurant which added just over three hours to their journey. What was most extraordinary was that they felt this was completely acceptable behaviour. I don't need to tell you where they came from. We don't ask that guests tell us their every movement, but it is just good manners to let us know if there are delays, in fairness most guests do tell us but it's the few that don't that we remember.

When our guests arrive, we have a large car parking area big enough for 8-10 cars. There is an extremely logical way to pull in and park which 97% of our guests do. They come up the drive and pull in towards a wall and continue to park parallel to get as many cars in as is required. On very busy occasions such as a wedding where we might have visitors doing hair and makeup, I will help organise the parking as some cars might get blocked in.

I completely understand that we are not all the same which is great, it's what makes us such a rich and diverse species, but I struggle to get my head around why 3% of our guests pull up and park at right angles so nobody else can park or we can only now get two cars where normally six would park. I understand that some people struggle with spatial awareness, I also understand that some people passed their driving test against all the odds, but I cannot understand when they get out of the car where they think anyone else might possibly park? What I have found out through experience when I politely ask them if they wouldn't mind moving their cars is that they never even considered anyone else, it genuinely never crossed their mind. One guest when I explained that parking at right angles meant we couldn't get enough cars in apologised profusely, turned his car round, and parked it at right angles in the other direction! In other words, in the same place but facing the other direction. I had to go out and direct him into the space. I found myself thinking about that line from Forest Gump, "Mama always said Stupid is as Stupid does".

When guests arrive, we try to meet them at their cars, introduce ourselves usually with the line, "Hi my name is Steve, welcome to Marlow House". I will invariably have Molly, our dog, with me; tail wagging away. I might be too demanding but what I would normally expect is, "Oh Hi, I am Rachel, and this is Gary," or similar. That happens about half the time, the other half is a mumbled 'Hi'.

I accept that some people are shy, or they don't see why they should share that sort of personal information with a stranger but given that they are going to be staying in our house and that we will probably have to speak to one another during their stay, it just makes it a bit more comfortable to be able to say hello. Perhaps I am overstepping the mark here and should really mind my own business but from a BnB owner's perspective it makes for a much more comfortable stay if you say hello and introduce yourselves.

I will always offer to carry guest's luggage into the house. Some guests are naturally prepared, they have their bags ready and know what they wish to bring in. Others go through what sometimes seems like an extraordinary process of selection with a multitude of bags, discussing whether they will need this or that. I can completely appreciate that they may not necessarily know everything they will need during their stay although they did pack to come; however, their car is only 40 yards from their room so popping back for something isn't the end of the world. We have had some guests who have taken 15 minutes or more to gather their belongings. This genuinely makes it quite embarrassing as small talk with someone you have just met usually gets exhausted after five minutes or so. In these instances, I usually say, "it's better if I don't stand over you while you are getting sorted, I will pop back in a few minutes". I then find a discreet place out of their way and wait until I think they are ready. This is not a great use of my time but all too often those guests wouldn't consider that.

Some guests travel very light, some come prepared in case they are offered late opera tickets or a chance to go potholing. One thing that is a constant is travellers from Australia and New Zealand. I always thought there was a maximum weight for luggage now under Health and Safety legislation to protect the backs of airport baggage handlers. I can only assume that Quantas and Air New Zealand have no such legislation. I can also understand that when travelling to the other side of the world and a different hemisphere there is a need to bring clothes for every eventuality particularly as we don't have many shops here but most of our Antipodean travellers are very experienced and do this type of journey all the time. It is barely an exaggeration to say that we need to hire in lifting equipment to get the cases out of the boot of the hire cars. I then look at the journey up our flights of stairs with some trepidation and wonder if my chiropractor will have a cancellation tomorrow. These cases cannot be carried in the normal way, they always have to be lifted overhead or on a shoulder, they are oversized and unbelievably heavy. Many of the travellers from down under are mature and I have no idea what they do when hotel staff don't lift their luggage for them.

I always have this discussion with our Antipodeans guests.

Steve: "With all your travelling and changing hotels, why don't you have a smaller overnight bag so that you can combine what you both need to make life easier for yourselves, it must be very difficult carrying your heavy cases all the time?"

Guests: "You know that's a really good idea, we should do that Doris/Edna/Sheila".

Perhaps we should carry a small line of overnight luggage to sell to these guests?

Over the four years we have been running our BnB we have worked out most of the questions that guests will ask us so that we have been able to condense the answers to these as well as other useful information onto a few sheets that we leave prominently in their rooms. You may recall in another chapter how I talked about emails and in the modern world many people now only have the capacity and interest to read the first two lines? That perplexing problem can also be translated into reading the information sheets. We have found that when taking guests to their rooms we have to run through some of the key tips written down as it is most likely that guests will not read them. Perhaps they are too busy, or it is just too exhausting. We leave the information there for the guests benefit in the same way we put some key information into their confirmation email or maybe we just do it for fun, who knows.

Any BnB or hotel owner will know that the most important thing for guests is not a comfortable bed, not a good night's sleep, not a friendly and welcoming ambience nor a spectacularly memorable breakfast. In this modern world the most critical and important requirement is the internet. Without this, life as we know it for most of our guests would cease to exist. It is almost guaranteed that the first request is, "What's the WiFi code?" The thought of being disconnected from the world for more than six or seven minutes between the car and their room is sometimes too much to cope with especially for the under 30s who visibly break out in a cold sweat if it doesn't upload immediately. We once had a pre-bridal wedding group here, and all ten of the girls were sat in the lounge in complete silence on their phones, this is the night before the wedding. I asked if they were all texting one another which didn't go down very well. They could have been looking after the bride making sure she was having a great time but clearly the Kardashians and ASOS were far more important.

We try to make sure our guests are settled in and invite them down to the guest lounge for a cup of tea.

Sometimes they might decide to have an afternoon cream tea. In this instance we ask them how long before they come down, so we can have it ready. They might say half an hour. This gives us ample time to prepare everything and put the scones in the oven to warm after 25 minutes. When the guests then don't come down for an hour or more we have the dilemma of re-heating the scones so that they may be potentially harder than we would like them to be or throw them away and prepare some new ones. We really don't mind what time our guests choose to come down, all we ask is that if you say something, please follow it through, as I said before Jane and I have to do everything, and we are happy to do it all willingly and with a smile, all we ask of our guests is to do what you say you are going to do.

Our guest lounge is full of useful information. Jane does an amazing job constantly gathering leaflets with almost everything there is to do locally and some of the spectacular things there are to do a little further away. All this information is laid out for guests to peruse and we have even created our own maps of local walks with great pubs.

We have a map to visit the nearby town which is detailed down to the nearest 10 metres. When followed it brings the guests into the loveliest part of the town where there is free on street parking and the most picturesque walk into the old part of the town. It also recommends the best cafes, places for lunch, walks, shops, just about everything you can acquire from having local knowledge. Most of our guests are thrilled with this and get the most out of their visits with us by utilising this information that has been gathered and honed over the 30 years that Jane and I have lived in this area.

I think you know what's coming. We have had guests return in the evening or even in the middle of the day thoroughly disappointed with their trip into the medieval Town.

Steve: “Did you enjoy your trip into Town?”

Guest: “No, not really.”

Steve: “I am sorry to hear that, why was that?”

Guest: “We had to pay £4 for car parking, the shops weren't very good, and we didn't have a very nice lunch, it was all a bit disappointing.”

Steve: “Didn't you follow the map?”

Guest: No, we put the satnav on, the lovely lady who lives inside it took us to the multi-storey car park.”

Steve: God give me strength (quietly to himself).

Anyone with a spark of intelligence knows that local knowledge can really make a trip. These guests never even found the town centre but stayed in the shopping centre wandering aimlessly around Marks & Spencer's and WH Smith's. They missed the 100 privately owned shops and boutiques that inhabit our wonderful Elizabethan shuts and passages, they missed the extraordinary architecture that makes it one of the most unspoilt towns in England. They had lunch in a Weatherspoon’s instead of visiting one of the many privately-owned bistros and restaurants that are putting our town on the map for gastronomy. How does the phrase go? 'You can lead a horse to water...'

Jane and I genuinely want to be helpful. We do this job because we enjoy it. We get to meet a lot of very interesting people and we enjoy the interaction. We do not have any kind of agenda apart from trying to make our guests' stay as pleasant as possible and to that end we have lots of information and experience to make that happen. Why anyone would think that the very nice satnav lady would know our local town better than us is a sad indictment on modern life. I am convinced that if she told the driver to turn right across the M6 and drive towards the oncoming traffic to knock eight minutes off the journey a few would do it.

Quite a few of our guests come to Marlow House because they are attending an event locally, more often than not this would be a wedding. We tend to know when the weddings are taking place, so we usually pre-empt the arrival with some questions about requirements for taxis. We have in the past booked taxis for guests to make their life easier only to find out that they left home too late and had to go directly to the wedding. Sometimes they wouldn't even tell us, and we would be having an awkward discussion with the taxi driver who has come from far away to collect the guests. We appreciate how the conversation must have been going in the car

Wife: "I told you we should have left earlier, I haven't even put my make up on, why did you go that way?"

Husband: "The satnav told me to."

Wife: "Well now we are going to be late, we will have to go straight to the wedding and it's all your fault. You will have to cancel the taxi.."

Husband: "I haven't got the number, it will be fine, he can pick up another fare."

We understand that our guests have other things on their mind other than letting the poor taxi driver know they aren't coming and wasting his time.

Because of this occasionally happening, we don't book the taxis directly anymore. We also don't run a courtesy taxi service to our local wedding venue. We were happy to do this when guests do what they say they are going to do. Some time ago we had eight guests staying all going to the same wedding; some of them knew one another. They asked to be picked up from the wedding at midnight. I duly arrived and, after much chasing, two of them finally came out at 12.20 the worse for wear. I needed to take them home and come back for the others. At 12.40 two more came out and said the others would get a taxi. At 1.10 I got a phone call saying they couldn't get a taxi (surprise surprise) so I went back to collect two more. Nobody could find the other two. They did manage to jump in somebody else's taxi, couldn't remember the address and arrived at 2.30. That was the last time we offered this service. Suffice to say not one of them offered to pay anything either.

We now email a list of taxi companies to our prospective guests making it very clear that we are in a rural location and that taxis will have to come from our local town. Part of the problem, and it is completely understandable is that 86% of the population live in conurbations and only 14% live in the countryside. With the advent of Uber and other online taxi services those that live in a large town or city are so used to a taxi being no more than 5 minutes away, it does not cross their mind that this may not be applicable everywhere. I can imagine them sitting in the Sahara Desert screaming at their phone because Uber says the taxi will be 17 hours.

Those observant readers will have spotted the problem with this last paragraph. Why were they sitting in the Sahara Desert? Is it that girl with the sense of humour in the satnav again? No, it's adding another line to the email making it most likely that it won't get read.

We have had so many guests arriving coming up the steps in a state of disarray, "the traffic was terrible", or "we couldn't find you", perhaps, "we didn't think it was this far"; oh yes, we get that a lot. As we show them to their rooms we always politely ask knowing the answer, "Have you booked a taxi?"

If there is a 100% correlation this is it:

Those that arrive late, dishevelled, in a state of disarray have not ordered a taxi.

This is one of life's great truths.

"Would you like us to book you one?" We feel we can now offer that as they are physically in our sight.

"Yes please, that would be great."

"When would you like it for?" already knowing the answer.

"5-10 minutes?"

At this point I attract their gaze to look outside at the open countryside full of rolling hills, cows grazing, lambs springing in the fields, a picture of bucolic delight devoid of modernisation.

"That might be a bit tricky given how rural we are, I did mention this in my email with the list of the taxi companies."

He looks at her, she looks at him.

Breaking the ice, I suggest that if they drive down to the wedding, get a taxi back then one of the other wedding guests can probably drive them back in the morning to collect their car or perhaps we will. They are hugely relieved at this piece of reasoning and 20-30 minutes later (5-10 was always far too optimistic) they head off clattering down the steps, she is looking very elegant if somewhat unsteady on her unfeasibly high heels, he dressed as though he is due in court, or in the Secret Service if it is sunny and he is wearing sun glasses. It is another universal truth that most women look at their best when dressed for a wedding whereas men generally look uncomfortable; smart but uncomfortable.

In our first year running the BnB we used to stay up waiting for guests to return, to let them in and make sure they were OK. The alcohol license at our local venue runs out at 12.30 so generally most guests are back by 1am in different states of sobriety. We changed three years ago and introduced security keypads meaning we didn't have to wait up. We were concerned about those that might struggle to remember their rooms or more logically to remember the code. We overcame this by giving them the code on a piece of paper which they then photographed on their phone. To date, and I am probably tempting fate, nobody has been unable to get in at night.

Breakfasts

We serve breakfast at Marlow House between 8 and 9.30. This isn't fixed, we don't run a totalitarian regime and can be very flexible when asked. We used to run breakfast from 8-10 but found breakfast sometimes running on until 11am.

In a perfect world we would like to think that serving breakfast from 8-9.30 means serving breakfast from 8-9.30. As with so many things in life perception is everything. Guests' interpretation of our breakfast timings arrive down between 7.30 and 9.45.

These are probably just semantics, I am sure the National Theatre will hold back the start of "Hamlet" for late arrivals, David Tennant sipping on his mineral water waiting for the last theatre goer to arrive.

We always ask our guests what time they would like breakfast as this gives us a little heads up in terms of preparation. If we only have 2 or 4 guests staying, we don't need to be up at 7 and ready for 8 if they say they want a late breakfast at 9.30.

To all users of Bed & Breakfasts reading this book, if there is one piece of BnB etiquette that I can implore you to adopt it is this:

If you say you are coming for breakfast at 8am please do not come down at 9.30, equally if you say you are coming for breakfast at 9am and then decide not to bother coming for breakfast at all, please can you let the BnB owner know? Let me explain:

There are three essential day to day functions in running the BnB in relation to looking after guests.

1) The Meet and Greet which we have covered.
2) Housekeeping, changing and preparing the rooms
3) Breakfasts, the staple of all good BnBs.

There are other elements like maintenance, marketing, PR etc which we will cover in another chapter.

Breakfast works by Jane and I preparing the table so that everything is just so, for when our guests come down. We work on the basis of being up at 7am getting ready for 8am or for whatever time guests have said they are coming down.

Once we are at that stage we wait. Actually, I wait, Jane walks Molly, I continue to wait. I would love to go out and creosote a fence or change the head gasket in the car, but I can't, I have to be ready for when our guests come down for breakfast and they said they were coming down at 8am. It's now 8.30am. I write a few emails, perhaps read an online newspaper and wait. Most guests are great, they do what they say they are going to do and we love them. They understand the relationship between human beings, one of mutual understanding and respect. We understand that we cannot all be the same, it makes for a more interesting and diverse life. It's 9 o'clock. The news has gone around on a perpetual loop, Steph McGovern is in danger of repeating herself. I consider having breakfast myself, but I know exactly how that will end up. The clock moves almost imperceptibly towards 9.30. Jane is back with Molly and gives me that knowing look.

At exactly 9.30 I start to clear away, but I am immediately stopped by Jane who was anticipating my impatience reminding me that I cannot really do that. I make a piece of toast and have my third cup of tea as the big hand swings round to the six and I hear voices coming through the guest lounge.

"Good Morning," they say chirpily.

"Good Morning," I reply. "Did you sleep well?"

"Oh yes, amazingly, it was so quiet, we didn't wake up until 8.30 and then just enjoyed the peace and quiet."

"Oh, that's lovely", I reply, "we wondered if you had to get anywhere early today when you asked for breakfast at 8 o'clock."

"We are normally up really early at home with the kids and work, it was lovely having a lie in."

These guests will then proceed to have a full English breakfast and leave the table at 10.45 making breakfast service almost 4 hours!

I cannot speak for all BnB owners but from personal experience this is my number one bugbear. If writing this book just makes one person think about this and changes their behaviour, then I will be a happy man.

I have spoken elsewhere about dietary requirements.

We cater for most needs and will do our very best to give guests what they need however we aren't mind readers. We went on a course but turned out to be really bad at it so we just cannot read people's minds and prefer to use the power of communication to find out if guests need something special whether that be gluten free, for a lactose intolerance, a fear of any foods with adjacent vowels or what has become known in our household as an aversion to anything orange which is more common than you might think.

Most guests with special dietary needs will make us aware in advance. Even though our request for information usually lies in line 5 or 6 of the welcome email making it useless as most people can't get past line 2, they will let us know of their own volition. After all, they experience this issue daily and know the inconvenience it can cause them and the restaurants if everyone is not made aware. It is just common sense. These guests will invariably bring their own gluten free bread, virgins' milk or tea bags filled with the ashes of Tibetan Monks.

Unfortunately, as we all know Common Sense is not distributed evenly. We have had many guests where I am at the point of running through the choices then tell us they have allergies and special requirements. We can always work round this, but it usually involves quickly defrosting vegan sausages or breads or something which then makes the timings of breakfasts more complicated if their partner doesn't have any aversions.

Please, just let us know even if it only gives us a few minutes' notice- please.

I talk at length about children in another chapter. Jane and I love all kids, it's the parenting that sometimes is problematic. Most parents are fantastic, but the reality is that many children like to be up early. On several occasions, we are laying the table and preparing breakfast with the children of guests around us usually with no sign of the parents. We are never sure if the children have just wandered down on their own or if the parents have held the door ajar and given them a gentle nudge. We don't really mind having the children down with us, it's not ideal but we are human. The problem is that we have no idea if the children have dietary issues. Can we take the chance of giving them an egg sandwich only to find out from an incensed mother that the child is bread intolerant and had an altercation with a chicken at the city farm and is now traumatised near eggs?

Parents, if you feel the need to subcontract your parenting please give us some parameters.

We take great pride in our breakfasts here at Marlow House as I would hope every BnB owner worth their salt would do as well. It is the singular thing that most guests remember their visit by. It isn't that difficult especially if you are doing it most days.

A good breakfast is nothing more than:
Great ingredients
Served hot and in a timely fashion
In an environment conducive to enjoying food
Ideally in good company

We serve our breakfasts in our Orangery. We call it an Orangery, it's just a posh conservatory. It is very light and bright and has spectacular views across the valley and over the hills. Certainly not the best view in the UK but if you are one of the 86% who live in a conurbation it looks mightily impressive.

Ingredients: we have spent some time on this and found out what guests like. Our bacon and black pudding come from a local pig farm and are smoked and cured there so the supply chain is very short. Our local butcher supplies our sausages, we have a free-range egg farm locally as well as a few of our own chickens. Tomatoes, mushrooms and beans come from our local supermarket as does our salmon. Jane makes a spectacular home-made granola using coconut oil. All our fruits and yoghurts also come from a local supermarket.

I have tried offering different sorts of breakfasts, but the most popular choices have come down to:

Our Full English Breakfast

Fry two good quality sausages on a high heat for 4-5 minutes in a little olive oil until brown on two sides then remove to a microwaveable dish.

In the same pan fry two rashers of bacon until almost done, during the last minute add a piece of black pudding. Put to one side.

In Olive oil and Oregano cook one whole tomato quartered.

In another pan sauté in butter 4 or 5 mushrooms, halved or quartered depending on the size.

Once the tomato and mushrooms are more or less cooked, microwave the sausages for two minutes. At the same time cook the eggs.

Scrambled eggs: Scramble 2 eggs with 20g of butter and stir constantly until cooked but not overdone.

Fried eggs: heat a little olive oil in two fried egg pans, these are so useful as the fried eggs come out a perfect shape. When the oil is hot, but not smoking, crack one egg in each and swirl to get the yoke centred then cook for 4 minutes to get a perfect fried egg. From Spring to Autumn, we are able to get a plentiful supply of double yokes from our local chicken farm. We can get these because supermarkets can’t take them. They are oversized so would require special packaging and supermarkets know that if they sold them as double yokes and one wasn't upon cooking, then Mrs Jones from Acacia Crescent would come back citing trauma. Sadly, this is why they don't appear in supermarkets where everything has to be consistent, which means all the more for us and our guests!

Poached eggs: These seem to be everyone's nemesis. Jane is a great cook but panics over poached eggs. A whole industry has evolved with poaching pans, pouches and goodness knows what else. Poached eggs are very straightforward. They are easier to do in spring to autumn when chickens get more outdoor time. This means that the whites hold better, and the yolks don't cook as fast but don't let that put you off having poached eggs in the winter it's just they may not be perfect every time. It does help if the eggs are as young as possible though not critical. And it also helps if the eggs have been kept in a cool place, once again not critical. Boil some water in a kettle. Have a 2" deep pan already on a heat and pour the boiled water in. Immediately crack two eggs into the pan bringing the cracked shell as close to the water as your hands will manage (the more you do this you will find yourself gently lowering the egg into the water). When you are starting out you can gently swirl each egg to get the white to cover the yoke, lots of posh restaurants do this, I don't tend to as I am often cooking 4-8 eggs at a time. Cook for three minutes roughly then turn the heat down leaving the eggs to remain in the warm water. The yokes won't cook too much further but the whites will continue to firm up. Use a big enough slotted spoon to get the eggs out, you can trim around the eggs with the spoon when you do this to tidy them. I sometimes leave the egg in the spoon for a moment before I plate up, so they are dry especially if I am putting them onto toast.

Top Tip: it doesn't pay to use the same poached egg water twice, always change it for better results between batches. I sometimes cook up to 6 eggs in one batch, it doesn't affect them.

Whilst the eggs are cooking you can microwave the baked beans and pop the toast or brioche in.

Start plating up the breakfast, sausages, black pudding and bacon around the edge, then the mushrooms and the tomatoes trying to keep a clean plate, wipe with kitchen towel if necessary, add the eggs in the middle when ready then finally the beans. I should have mentioned that the plates should all be warmed in the oven whilst cooking takes place including the plate for toast. Full English tastes best when served piping hot.

I have a thing about plates being hot and mine are sometimes too hot. I always warn our guests that, "The plates are very hot, beyond inquisitive hot." Most guests take notice but occasionally someone will have to check, this is always "a man of a certain age" whom I will talk about in more detail later.

Two years ago, full English was easily our most popular breakfast. It still is on a Sunday morning, but we have noticed a big change in people's dietary habits. Our purchase of sausages has probably halved in the last year, eggs remain constant but we use a lot more salmon.

Salmon & Scrambled eggs

We have tried Salmon from many different suppliers and it is hard to beat Aldi. The Salmon is full of flavour and from a food preparation perspective the slices come away from one another very nicely making it easy to plate up. I always fleck the scrambled eggs with salmon as I feel it runs the flavour through the eggs. Naturally lemon and black pepper enhance this dish and served with a lovely granary toast. We use Sainsbury's *Taste the difference* with seeds, it's our personal preference.

Our signature breakfast is **mushroom, bacon & brie on brioche with a poached egg on top**. It's very simple but surprisingly delicious. Slice some mushrooms and sauté in a pan in butter with plenty of thyme. Fry a couple of slices of good quality bacon in a little olive oil. When the bacon is cooked cut into small pieces, mix these in with the mushrooms and add some brie cubed or sliced, cook for a couple of minutes then leave to melt together. At the same time boil a pan and cook a poached egg as described before. Pop a slice of brioche, which you can toast straight from the freezer, into the toaster. Plate up by arranging the mixture as best you can on the slice of brioche in the middle of the plate then spoon the poached egg on top and finish off with ground black pepper. It is a delightful combination.

Very popular is our **Eggs Benedict**. There are many variations of this and we are no exception. We steam a little baby spinach whilst frying off two good slices of bacon and poaching an egg. Pop two slices of brioche into the toaster. When everything is cooked split the spinach between the two brioches, season well, add a good spoonful of Hollandaise sauce to each pile of spinach, then two slices of bacon on one toast and the egg on the other. A few good turns of the pepper grinder and delicious. The sweetness of the brioche with the saltiness of the bacon really makes this dish and offers a nice variation to something that many people have had before.

We also offer **Blueberry Pancakes**, simple to make and very delicious, always popular with the children but parents often end up ordering some once they see their children's. Mix flour, milk and an egg and whisk until smoothish, I just do this quickly with a fork. Add some baking powder which makes them lovely and light. Melt some butter in a small pan, I use the same ones that I fry eggs in as they give a lovely shape. Pour the melted butter into the mix. Spoon a dollop of mixture into the still hot pan which is coated with the remains of the butter. Arrange a dozen blueberries into the mixture and put back on the heat, about four minutes one side, flip then another two minutes. Put a knife through the pancake middle to see if it is cooked through. Arrange on a plate then drizzle maple or golden syrup in diagonal lines for dramatic effect and top with sprinkled icing sugar then serve. These are very delicious and everyone without exception has a second one. Our record has been five to one guest.

Our guests are really surprised at the choices we offer but actually there is a lot of crossover and it works very well for us in the kitchen which is just as well as our kitchen and dining area is open plan, so they can see everything I am doing.

Our reviews tell us that guests love our range of breakfasts. Of course, we can offer other combinations, mixing and matching but we have found that these choices satisfy almost everyone.

That's a great breakfast in a great room with lovely views served hot and in a timely fashion. The only unknown is the mood and conversation at the table and as already said, this can vary enormously from group to group.

The difference between a mediocre breakfast and a great one nearly always comes down to the interaction between our guests, if we have some gregarious, chatty guests, breakfast usually gets off to a flying start, others prefer to keep themselves to themselves whilst others are just not sociable creatures. The dynamic also varies dramatically if children are there, especially babies. Little ones always dominate breakfasts. There is the paraphernalia, high chair, bibs and so forth plus the inevitable different breakfast or "he/she will share ours". New babies and young children are clearly wonderful, they are our future and something that should be appreciated, enjoyed, and revelled upon but please parents, they aren't the centre of everyone's world. It seems that parents of little ones feel the need to shoehorn their children into the centre of everything whether the other guests want that or not. There are the inevitable niceties, "Oh how lovely, what's his or her name, how old, does he/she sleep through." Here is another unspoken truth, after the niceties most guests just want to get on with their breakfast in peace and quiet, perhaps some polite chat but generally they don't want to hear about little Johnny's diet, his amazing feat with the baby stroller and that hilarious story with the ducks at the park. Here in the UK, we are all too polite, except for this author clearly, to say anything and we will ooh and aah and coo until we can't coo anymore but had our guests wanted to spend the whole of breakfast talking to a one year old they would have brought their own.

It is very difficult when you are in the eye of a storm or in this case drenched in the sunlight of a new born to realise that those around you might not be as enthusiastic at least not beyond the first five minutes. It's just an observation and Jane will probably kill me for saying so.

As the host it is always a tricky moment getting the conversation going. There are no fixed rules for deciding if disparate pairs or groups of people will get on when thrown together, we understand that. On occasions they have gotten on so well that they have become friends, gone out for dinner together in the evening and even returned later as a foursome but this is rare. All we can hope for as hosts is that our guests find each other's company vaguely enjoyable and are prepared to engage in some polite conversation and this happens most of the time.

Our table sits ten people, we can add leaves to sit up to 20. Generally, we are seating 10-14 for breakfast. We never know what time everyone will come down as I have alluded to previously. In a perfect world everyone would come down with gaps of ten minutes to allow us to make each breakfast fresh, the tricky part comes when everyone arrives together which happens more often than you might imagine. A statistician would work out the probability of six different couples having never met before having a window of opportunity spread over 90 minutes all arriving simultaneously at ten past nine. I imagine the odds would be quite long, but it happens all the time. We don't mind, we offer the window of ninety minutes and our guests have paid so it is their prerogative and almost without exception they are happy to wait whilst their breakfast is cooked fresh. It helps that we have an open plan kitchen/dining area, so I can chat to them and they can see the progress. Some people may feel this is not an ideal situation. Friends and other BnB owners have said they couldn't cook knowing that the guests could be watching them. I have never found this to be a problem, I can listen in on the conversation, throw in an opinion occasionally, some may say regularly, too regularly perhaps, and it certainly keeps me on my toes as there is nowhere to hide. Guests may feel they can’t speak as openly as they may have wanted to but that suits us too although it is amazing how quickly they forget we are there and let their guards drop. From a guests' perspective I think it is quite a good thing being able to see what the chef is up, at least you know the food has been meticulously prepared and hasn't ended up on the floor at any time.

One thing that is a challenge for us is when guests come down and decide where to sit at the table. There is one end of the table that affords all the views out to the valley, this tends to be pole position. The next guests down will invariably not want to sit directly next to those guests. That is human nature and is fine, in some respects in very polite England it would be a little strange to come and sit next to another couple when there are eight other seats to choose from, however there is clearly some considered decision making which makes for amusing viewing.

Imagine this scenario. Couple one have come down to breakfast and chosen pole position sitting at the head of the table, masters of all they survey. They probably already have their tea and coffee and perhaps by now also have their full English and a salmon and scrambled eggs in front of them. Couple two now come down and see The Orangery for the first time and have one of the most perplexing of British dilemmas which other nationalities don’t seem to have at all. They don’t really want to sit next to two people they may have bumped into on the stairs or in the car park but equally they don’t want to sit at the other end of the table for fear of appearing rude. What is the appropriate gap to ensure a degree of privacy without causing offence? The second couple will look at each other discussing it openly for polite company but utilising all the shared experience of their relationship subliminally to decide where to sit. In their hearts they would like to be on the other side of the table, but they know that might appear rude at worst, awkward at best. They move around the table leaning over the backs of the chairs, he with both hands on the chair, she is averting her gaze and then they settle for the two seats along from the first couple with a gap of one chair. This is the acceptable seating gap as defined by 'How We Built the Empire' published 1863 next to the chapter 'How to address a stranger in a sauna in Rangoon.'

The next guests arrive a few minutes later and go through the same process leaving one pair of seats and two single seats. It is an easier decision for them as a precedent has been already been made. It is at this point that I must decide what to do. Do I hope that the first couple finish before the last couple arrive so that a "pair" of seats become available? This means that I must clear away their places and reset them even though there are two unused places perfectly clean or do I pre-empt and suggest that if everyone moved along one then all of the guests could sit at the table.

This decision is influenced by the "chatability" factor something that is truly unique to BnBs that dine *en famille.* If the conversation is flowing and the guests realise that there is an opportunity to have a good time I will ask that question and dress it up to make it jovial. If the group has not gelled at all and is sitting in silence which rarely happens, then I will run the gauntlet and hope that the first couple have indeed finished. We have had some breakfasts run on past 11am where guests have got on so well that they lose track of time and talk about anything and everything but if there is a chill wind and everything is so quiet that you can hear a sausage drop then breakfasts tend to be swift. To date out of over 1000 breakfast services I have only had the experience a handful of times of a couple arriving to find the only remaining seats are on opposite sides of the table. In those instances, we offer the late arrivals tea and coffee in the guest lounge which they are relieved to accept.

It is truly amazing that, almost without exception, nobody ever thinks about what might happen if everyone leaves a gap, it's up there with spatial awareness and generally considering others.

I said earlier that a huge bugbear of mine and probably other BnB owners is guests not coming down at the time they say or not coming down at all. Here comes my other personal irritant. We don't have printed menus here at Marlow House, I don't know why, we don't really like our breakfast table to look like a BnB table, we try and keep everything here more like just staying at someone's house, it's how we like to do it and most of our guests like it as well, obviously not everyone, as we all know it is impossible to please everyone, so we don't have menus. This means that I tell our guests what is available for breakfast. This is one of the rare occasions in the BnB/Guest relationship where the balance of power switches to the BnB owner. I can say exactly what I want, I can leave things out or I can gently guide guests towards something I want to cook that day if I so choose. The reality is I am so used to cooking all the items on the menu that it is very rare for me to leave anything out although if there are any children I do wax lyrical about the pancakes as I cannot bear waste and have seen far too many children leave the majority of a full English Breakfast. It's not the cost, everything has been budgeted; it's just that right now there are lots of people struggling financially so I hate to see waste that is so unnecessary.

So, I enjoy holding all the power for a minute to a minute and a half. At that point I know I have lost it again and for a moment my heart sinks. I have listed the breakfast menu earlier with all the cooking instructions but in case you have forgotten, here goes.

"So, this morning I can offer you lots of lovely cooked things. Perhaps Archie and Olivia would like Blueberry pancakes or for a special treat I could make them with strawberries and Maple Syrup (children's eyes light up ... generally), perhaps some salmon and scrambled eggs, eggs Benedict Marlow House Style, our house speciality of mushrooms, bacon and brie on brioche with a poached egg on top and of course a Full English Breakfast Staffordshire style."

Now perhaps I am too familiar with the menu, but I can't see too much there to have to consider. If it's a Sunday 75% of guests will order a full English, after all as your doctor will tell you it doesn't count on a Sunday. Otherwise there tends to be a reasonably even split between the choices depending upon any emphasis I might stress on the day. Half of guests know exactly what they want, they were probably thinking about it from the moment they opened their eyes, another 30% have listened intently and something has appealed. There is then another 10% who need to have some variations to the options, they can do this because they do this in London all the time. That leaves about one in ten people who:

1) Do not follow my particular dialect
2) Were so amazed at the incredible choice they have become a quivering wreck
3) Cannot string a sentence together unaided

Those fleeting seconds where I held all the power in my hand seem like an eternity ago. Do I stand there like a pillar of salt waiting for their hard drive to reboot? Do I gently encourage them into a decision? Do I sympathise with their partner and give them a knowing hug?

I have now learnt to regain some control by saying, "I don't want to stand over you whilst you are deciding, I can come back in a few minutes or just give me a shout."

This invariably triggers the response:

"Could you just go through the list again please?"

This usually does the trick, but I have had a few guests who still couldn't decide. I think the record was about 12 minutes.

I always joke with them by saying something like, "How did you ever manage to buy a house?" or, "How did you choose your partner?"

It breaks the ice after something that started out as amusing becomes embarrassing for the whole table.

I don't think cooking breakfasts is difficult but many other people do, as I have said before, it is just practice and the only slightly tricky thing is timing. When one person orders a breakfast and the other decides 12 minutes later do I start the first one knowing they will be served separately or make the decision to wait, in other words playing to the lowest common denominator which drives me nuts?

All this can be overcome with some gentle banter, at least the joking around the breakfast decisions breaks the ice and gets everyone engaged so still not as bad as the chilly iced table of silence that can occasionally occur.

There is a whole chapter about the unusual things that happen here at Marlow House and guest stories, however I shall regale some of the funny and slightly odd guest stories around breakfast as this seems the appropriate place to do so.

Weird and wacky requests

We don't get that many odd requests for food. For sure we get a proportion of guests with 'medical' or 'dietary issues' many of which are geographically based, others that were probably diagnosed by their GP looking for a quiet life, I am certain that some are absolutely genuine and fulfil a need.

"I can't have any of my food touching."

This isn't as rare as you might think. We have had ten

or more guests who cannot have their beans touching any of their food. Pandered, weird, wacky, however you might wish to describe the illogicality of it, it's true. I can't really talk as I had a personal phobia about celery until my mid-30s.

We had one guest who told me, "I can't have any of my food touching." I naturally said, "your beans can't touch anything?"

The young lady replied, "No, I can't have any of the items on the plate touching one another.."

One of the problems with being irreverent is that I just can't accept things that I think are ridiculous so when I served her breakfast to her it resembled a hilltop fortress in the Sinai with each item separated from the next by a low castellated wall made of toast. This was greeted by roars of laughter around the table and fortunately she also saw the funny side. I never thought to ask if any of the eggs or bacon could touch the toast. She ate it all and thanked me, so I suppose it was OK.

If we have a jovial group I will thoroughly engage and have a joke with them. When they ask what is in the full English I will run through the ingredients and then add Doner kebab or profiteroles at the end. One chap who was part of a group of young farmers said he wanted everything. I double checked that he meant everything. His full English was accompanied on the same plate by Haribo, chocolate digestives and a Mars bar.

Two guests who were built for comfort and not speed when they arrived the evening before filled in their guest forms and under the line "Special Dietary Requirements" wrote "We like big portions, just letting you know for breakfast tomorrow."

It is hard to know exactly what their expectations were, "big" is very subjective. However, I could see by their ample frames that they hadn't reached that proportion by having average size breakfasts so I up scaled on the day. They each had:

3 sausages
3 large rashers of bacon
3 eggs
2 tomatoes
8 mushrooms
A large helping of beans
2 black puddings
2 rounds of toast.

To be honest it was embarrassing for the other guests. As they started to finish I politely asked them as I do with all our guests if I could get them anything else. The gentleman was clearly struggling as he pointed out they had had a very big meal the night before and couldn't finish all of his. His wife however saw this as an opportunity, sliding his plate across to hers and requesting just a couple more slices of toast. They had both already consumed two full bowls of fruit and cereal and a whole jug of orange juice. It was truly epic and reminded me very much of *The Meaning of Life* by Monty Python and "Would Sir like a wafer-thin mint?" Obesity crisis, what crisis? I had never previously heard a chair let out a sigh of relief when she lifted herself up to head off for her next meal.

Cultures differ to one another we all know that. I have been fortunate enough in previous careers to have travelled widely and so I like to think I have a level of experience and understanding to accept all cultures here at Marlow House and embrace them.

A mother and daughter from China visited us. The mother was of what we might call standard build. Her daughter however was vast, she may at one time have had two or three siblings but probably ate them. The mother told us that she was over here to enrol her daughter in a college to learn English as she would be getting involved in their family manufacturing business. It can be difficult eating the food in another country, I completely understand that. When I first visited China in the year

2000 it was very difficult to find milk products and yet now China is the world's biggest consumer of milk. By the end of a three-week trip I was craving chocolate and I don't even eat that much chocolate but there were no dairy products at all in China at that time. In fact, the Chinese I met said that we Westerners used to smell like milk, which they found difficult. It reminded me of when I was a child and my mother said our new neighbours smelled of curry, it's just different cultures, nothing more. Anyway, the daughter aged about twenty asked for everything to eat and spent an hour picking her way through it all using five or six plates as she moved food from one to another. They got up and left the breakfast table and I felt relieved. Ten minutes later she returned with two of the silver containers (the large ones) that you get from a Chinese restaurant or takeaway. This was food she had bought previously and kept tucked away for a little snack. When served on a plate it looked enormous, in fact it was on two full size dinner plates. She returned to the table (I had to re-lay a setting as by now we were well past 11am) and she sat there patiently for another 45 minutes finishing both off. It was extraordinary but equally quite impressive. Sadly, this girl had no social graces at all, I imagine she was an only child and had always been spoilt with her parents doing everything for her.

It is one thing when parents send their children down to breakfast before them or when they make the children the centre of the whole breakfast experience, but the other side is when they completely ignore their children. This can also be quite painful especially when I am cooking in the same space. On a few occasions the children, bored because they are ignored by their parents, come up to where I am cooking on a six ring SMEG commercial cooker and stand with me or sit on the floor at my feet. This is tricky as I have no option but to ask the parents to move the children out of harm's way, which they always do immediately but within a minute or two the children are back. The repeated conversation then becomes embarrassing because clearly the parents have no parenting abilities or just don't care. On three occasions I have had to speak to the children myself in a firm tone which naturally I do not want to have to do but it is dangerous, so I have no choice. Even at that point it goes straight over the parents' heads who are more interested in their mobile devices or staring out of the window.

One of the strangest things that can happen at breakfast and it has happened on half a dozen occasions is when guests want to come and see how breakfast is being cooked. I blame the Saturday morning cookery shows, "Can't cook won't cook," "Dinner in a jiffy," "A feast from bits left in the fridge" and others.

Some people seem to think it is perfectly acceptable behaviour to stand next to the chef to watch and ask about the ingredients and how to do this or that. I wonder how Gordon Ramsey would react if a diner wandered in to the kitchens of The Petrus or The Savoy Grill and asked Gordon how he got his pancakes so light? I would like to think that our guests who have done this over the years felt my awkwardness, perhaps it was a test, I wonder if I passed?

We are often asked for our recipes especially when we cook evening meals which is fine, we are happy to provide these and some tips, but we aren't a Michelin star establishment, just well-prepared food with good ingredients and a bit of thought. We like to try new restaurants and pick up ideas, but we do that by observation of what we are eating rather than heading off to the kitchen to stand next to the chef. Dear guests, as part of the etiquette at least please ask before coming up to the kitchen to join in.

When our guests arrive we always welcome them to Marlow House and tell them that whilst they are here that "our home is your home". We always felt this was a nice thing to say to make them feel more relaxed so that they can enjoy their stay to the maximum and to this day we still say that. We are surprised though when some guests, almost always those with children take it quite literally.

I had been preparing breakfasts when a mother came through with a bag of rubbish and said as she put it in the bin, "Is it OK to put this in here, it's a few nappies and other things?". She then proceeded to mix the formula milk at the sink and put it in the microwave, without asking or even saying a word. We are thrilled that they feel so relaxed and maybe it is our Britishness, but I did find it quite odd and it hasn't been an isolated incident, this has happened on a handful of occasions. It's all about perception, what one person finds acceptable may not be considered so by someone else. We would have been most happy to prepare the formula milk and warm it for them, it just felt odd going ahead without asking.

We try not to get hung up on how people behave regarding etiquette. We appreciate that people do different things from different parts of the UK. It is quite natural for a girl from Liverpool to walk around in her rollers all day whereas a Londoner would consider that odd. We see people using cutlery in different ways, but it is just the way they were brought up, what they saw around them as information absorbing children. Some might regard this as class distinction, but we are all just a reflection of our upbringing. However, something that makes it quite tricky being involved in the service sector is how people leave their cutlery when they are finished.

This might seem extraordinarily pedantic, but it is unnecessarily difficult for us when guests finish eating and leave their cutlery strewn across their plates. This is increasingly common with young people. The problem for us is that many youngsters will leave part of their food on their plate for whatever reason and then leave their cutlery at all kinds of angles. The difficulty is that we just don't know if they have finished or not.

We like to quietly go about our work so that we do not

have to disturb guests especially if they are in conversation, but we find ourselves increasingly having to ask guests if they have finished before we clear their plates away. It isn't a big thing, but cutlery brought together in the middle of the plate always used to be a universal indicator that the meal was finished making it very simple for the staff to clear away.

Another unspoken truth about running a BnB, and this applies to life in general, really is the timing of things. It is an absolute guarantee that right at the height of breakfast service, usually when the eggs are almost ready and need to be watched, the phone will ring. This will invariably be an enquiry as to availability. Perhaps people looking to book think the most likely time a BnB owner will be in is during breakfast service. If that is the case, do they not think that might be a busy time? Of course, that isn't the case at all, nobody thinks about things like that, it is just a convenient time to call. They have probably just read their emails, seen an invite and think they want to get the accommodation sorted as soon as possible. If you are ever in a position to be booking a room at a BnB, 8.30-10am is the busiest time for BnB owners. They have generally worked out their communication systems, so you can contact them any time of day anyway, that's how modern businesses run.

Another anomaly of the service industry in general is that the service is provided with payment often coming at the end. Once again this is where the balance of power is very lopsided. We will have provided everything before the guest has to pay. This has changed in the last year, we now insist on a deposit beforehand. We never used to but now that it is more commonplace and indeed becoming set in the public psyche, as I have previously mentioned, that you can book somewhere so that you have something in the bank that can later be cancelled, we feel we have no choice but to ask for a deposit refundable up to seven days before arrival.

We have never had a situation where guests have been

unhappy and not wanted to pay. When we started, friends of ours said that we would have to write down car registration numbers because they had heard that guests abscond without paying. We have never experienced this at all although recently we had one couple who left in the middle of the night without paying because he had had a terrible row with his family. We did get paid the following day. We had a period when everyone was moving away from cash payments to credit cards and we were a little slow in getting a card machine. During that period, we had several guests who had no means of paying but they always settled their bill as soon as they arrived home by online banking.

So, I am pleased to say that we have never had a bad debt in terms of guests staying and then leaving without paying.

Our check out time when guests are departing, is by 11am which invariably means that some will want to leave and settle their bill during breakfast service. Most successful husband and wife teams that run BnBs work out their roles and responsibilities. If they do that well it can be a very enjoyable way to make a living and leave yourselves lots of free time. In our business, we will lay the table together. Jane then walks Molly whilst I cook and serve breakfast, Jane then comes back in plenty of time to take payments and say farewell to our guests. This works brilliantly for us and for our guests, it is relaxed and a perfect end to their stay. It goes wrong when guests don't tell us they need to leave early. On some occasions, I have been in the middle of cooking breakfast at 8.30 when guests have come in to the kitchen and said they would like to pay. No matter how well prepared we are this has the potential to be tricky. It is Sod's law that when these guests ask to pay, three or four breakfasts are just about to be plated up. It is at that precise moment the phone goes for a booking and by some extraordinary coincidence this is also the moment that BT decide our internet needs tweaking and goes off. Jane! Help! This has only happened a couple of times and on both occasions, I have had to say that we will send them an email and they can pay online which they both duly did as soon as they arrived home. One couple were so mortified that they couldn't settle the bill there and then that they explained in enormous detail how they would never normally not pay, that their word was their bond and how they were thoroughly trustworthy. No amount of appeasement from my end could assuage their guilt. The result was that four breakfasts went in the bin and had to be started again. Once again this was quite extraordinary as they had found me in the kitchen with eight guests sat at the table waiting for their breakfasts, but their needs were clearly greater.

I hope that my ramblings are an insight for any potential guests as to how BnB and Hotel owners perceive guest etiquette. If guests were able to have some insight into how hotels and guest houses work everything might run a little smoother.

CHAPTER 7
ONLINE DISCOUNT GROUPS

Not that many years ago Groupon arrived in the UK. This was a website that came from America. In its original guise, anyone could ask for a price, for example for a fridge freezer. The price might have been $300 but a manufacturer or wholesaler would offer it for $200 if 100 people could order one. As this business grew and came to the UK the model changed and companies would offer a product at a rock bottom price usually based on a minimum order, in other words the price would entice the purchase rather than the need enticing the price.

There are so many great ideas that capture the imagination but then run out of steam as the commercial realities bite.

When we started the BnB we ran a Groupon promotion to get going. You can imagine the problem of starting a BnB, in terms of raw logistics, you really need to be around all day in case you get a booking but initially until your marketing gets going bookings can be few and far between. We thought that by tapping into Groupon's enormous database we could quickly get some bookings, so we could, quite frankly, learn what we were doing. We knew that we would have to give a significant discount to make it appealing, but we accepted this as part of our marketing budget. We didn't know at that stage what the market rate for our rooms should be, so we came up with some numbers and then negotiated with Groupon.

Clearly our offer was very good as we were inundated with bookings. We quickly found out over the next three months that we were far too cheap and were offering far too much for the money. We didn't mind that we weren't really making any money as it was great experience and putting us on the map. Five years ago, when we started, TripAdvisor was so market dominant in the reviews area and potential guests were using TripAdvisor as a key source of information. We accepted the very thin margins and lots of work which meant our guests were incredibly happy as we had really exceeded their expectations which in this industry is always a good thing to do. So, many guests left glowing reviews which helped us enormously and really got us going.

There were two major downsides that we hadn't really considered. The first was the amount of work involved to satisfy the expectations of our Groupon customers who really like lots of meals with their deals. We love cooking and we love doing things well. Our guests were enjoying three course meals with canapés on white linen served in the Orangery or, if the weather was good out on the terrace, but paying very little for it. By the end of the promotion we were exhausted as we had been doing this more or less every day and night. We put it down to experience and a trade-off for putting us on the map. Despite almost everyone leaving reviews saying what an amazing time they had, there were parts of the review where they could measure cleanliness, how friendly the hosts were and value for money. Some guests still marked us down on value for money, probably as their own strategy for continually putting downward pressure on prices.

The other unintended consequence was that whenever anyone searched for Marlow House (because as recently as three or four years ago, guests would search us out by name whereas now 90% of bookers go directly to booking agents like booking.com), they would find us on Google and the Groupon offer would be there. There were two disadvantages. The first being that they could see the Groupon deal and would look for something similar from us but the second was that at that time Groupon had become synonymous with discounting and the lower end of the market. This really came back to bite us when we tried to join an upmarket online website; Alistair Sawdays. We were declined. It had been our first setback and it was quite a shock at the time, we felt a little deflated after all our hard work.

We have not run a promotion with Groupon since for these reasons. It took a long time before our association with Groupon dropped to page two of Google, hardly anyone looks beyond page one.

We have subsequently run promotions for the quiet months with Wowcher, Secret Escapes and Voyage Prive. Wowcher really was a similar proposal to Groupon and we only did that once. Secret Escapes has worked very well for us in the past and has really helped us during the quiet months of January, February and March. We have been happy in the past to run really good deals to encourage guests to come and stay with us. Our view is that it is a quiet period and if we can get guests to come, especially midweek, we will really make it worth their while.

In this instance we see a mutual benefit working with Secret Escapes as this means we can utilise their database of discerning clients who want to visit lovely hotels and BnBs but would like a discount for travelling during low season. Unfortunately, as I have mentioned before, everything in life is about perception.

This is very much our perception, our view. Secret Escapes and all the other booking companies are suffering from traveller fatigue and an increasingly crowded marketplace. The relationship has also altered dramatically as it has done with Booking.com and the other OTAs. As companies grow they are always subject to shareholders demands and pressure on profits. Rather than being able to develop a symbiotic relationship with their suppliers so that everybody wins they must scramble for market share. How do they get the pool of potential guests to book with them rather than any of the other online agents and discount companies? By offering more for less. Does this mean that they themselves take a thinner margin? Sadly not. The more for less must be constantly met by the hotel industry who are already under enormous pressure from the OTAs taking 15%+ from an increasing number of bookings.

The 'Deals Companies' not only want the hotels and BnBs to offer food within the offer but also weekends and high season. During a discussion with one such company they insisted on being able to offer all the weekends to their customer base at a discount of 40% and then their 23% commission on top. When I said we couldn't do that they informed me that they had so many hotels queuing up to run offers that they also wanted £2000 up front even to place the offer. Naturally we declined. Three months later they were ringing me desperate to get us to run an offer with them. One thing we do know is that with technology things change very rapidly.

We no longer run any offers with these companies preferring to email our past guests with great deals. We were being invited into a race to the bottom that sadly many hotels and BnBs are having to enter because their fixed costs are too high, their bankers are unsupportive or if they are in a town centre they are being squeezed by those hotels that choose to play this mad game and are capturing the lion's share of the bookings; but at what cost? It will be a short-lived pyrrhic victory. As we found to our cost when we ran the very first Groupon promotion that was so crazy busy (being the halcyon days of the promotion companies, most are now struggling) the wear and tear element only happens sometime after the promotion has run. Too many guests coming through relentlessly takes a real toll on the fabric of the business, physical in terms of carpets, linen, furnishings and mentally in terms of the staff's wellbeing.

It is extraordinary how quickly these new businesses and new marketing models come and go. The problem with all these offers is that it drives the public perception of pricing ever downwards and ultimately there is always a price to pay by somebody somewhere.

In the 1990s I had a little manufacturing business. Like so many other business people I saw the opportunity to have everything made abroad, in China and other places. I 'offshored' all of it and for a few years enjoyed a tremendous advantage and did very well. Of course, it only lasted a short while until most manufacturers did the same and the goods we were importing ended up commoditised and we were all competing on price. All our design elements were copied, and the general psyche of our customers moved away from quality, design, and durability to price. Here in the UK we had twenty years of deflation where everything just seemed to get cheaper and everyone enjoyed a higher standard of living because all that we bought just seemed to get cheaper. Everyone could afford garden furniture sets, flat screen TVs, coffee machines, smart phones, things that had been unaffordable just became commonplace. At the same time wages didn't need to rise, employers could see that everyone's standard of living was rising due to deflation without having to pay out any more money. Many company's margins increased very quickly as they closed their UK manufacturing operations and sent it all abroad selling off their premises. Of course, this is all short termism that has all come home to roost as the cheap labour abroad is no longer cheap because their own economies have developed, and most good ideas and USPs have been copied and devalued.

The OTAs and the deal sites had the same model driving down the price of hotel rooms allowing more people to be able to stay away and have mini breaks and treats but generally at the cost of the hotel owner. As recently as the 1970s and 80s, stays away in hotels were the preserve of business people or the wealthy and the affluent middle classes, today so many more people are living what would have been considered then a millionaire's lifestyle.

There are an awful lot of hotel owners who don't yet realise what has happened. They have remained busy and benefitted from low cost labour due to high levels of immigration and have thus kept going but valuations of hotels for sale tell the real story. It has become very hard to make profits from a hotel if there is a lot of borrowed money, there are just too many downward pressures on pricing whilst costs are now constantly rising.

This is a period that business schools will run courses on in due course, explaining the impact that technology had sitting in the middle and giving the impression of being a panacea to everyone but turning out to be a cancer; destroying profits without really adding any value except to their own shareholders. I have the utmost respect for these companies, they are far cleverer than I am, spotting the opportunity and seeing it through. I am sure that the intellectually gifted founders of these businesses had some altruism and weren't solely driven by money, they saw the opportunity to rationalise a fragmented industry bringing clarity and organisation and with it the chance for bookers to get the best price and for hotels to get more bookings. But that was a few years ago. Most of these businesses have fallen into the hands of another very clever group of people, the venture capitalists, those who cannot come up with the original ideas nor bring them to market, but who can see the opportunity for enormous wealth by exploiting the proven model. There is no altruism, no concern for the greater good. There is no hypocrisy either, this is not what they set out to do and they have never deluded anyone that it was. These shadowy people who sit in the background know how to maximise their profits and there is always a cost. It doesn't help that their goals and timeframe are usually as short as possible. The wreckage and broken lives en-route is of no concern to them just the financial reward at the end. This is the free market economy.

Before the technology revolution Governments understood what Monopolies were, how they could control a market and influence pricing. Laws were introduced to inhibit such activities. That was twenty years ago. We now live in a new world, a digital world that is difficult to really comprehend, that moves so fast and influences every aspect of our lives, fake news, elections, even our own social standing and a great phrase now exists; "the inside of your own life never looks as appealing as the outside of someone else's" to describe the pain that Facebook causes so many people.

So many technology companies are monopolies but not in the sense that history understands. Economics teachers will tell their students about monopolies in industry dominating a market place so that they can move pricing to create unfair advantages by their dominance. This market dominance is clear for all to see in so many respects, but it can't be managed politically. If the telecoms industry only had one player and the price of phone calls seemed to be rising too fast, the Government could intervene and break up that monopoly insisting that other players could have access to the infrastructure that the monopoly had enjoyed. It is all reasonably transparent.

What happens when a technology company creates something that is unique and becomes so market dominant that it is virtually impossible for any other player to compete? In theory a Government should be able to apply the same logic and laws to break that monopoly. The telecoms company probably had their head office in Slough, their sales offices in Swindon and Birmingham and reported all their accounting directly to the stock market in the UK. Their business model was absolutely proven to be in the UK. and could come under UK law and be scrutinised by Parliament. The technology companies are global, their power is in their operating systems and their connection to their customers. It has proven very difficult if not impossible to determine where their businesses are truly domiciled, where their revenue comes from and where they can be taxed let alone legislated against. Profits for the most successful are mind blowing and some of these companies have more cash off shored than the annual GDP of many countries.

What does any of this have to do with hotels and BnBs? There are two main points. Firstly, the most successful become industry dominant like Booking.com. This means that their suppliers become increasingly reliant on them which makes them very vulnerable to price increases. Booking.com isn't really interested in offering the widest possible choice to guests, that doesn't particularly help their business model. They might like to give the impression of being omnipresent and benevolent offering their guests everything that is available but all they are really interested in is rooms being booked. If the bottom 20% of hotels went bankrupt and closed that wouldn't bother them at all as it would drive the requirement for rooms through fewer suppliers. Booking.com could then argue that they were helping fill those hotels by getting them higher occupancy, after all the hotel industry works on the calculation of 'occupancy multiplied by room rate less running costs'.

Larger hotels would benefit from smaller hotels closing and in the short term would be prepared to pay a premium for this to happen. This means Booking.com could increase their base fee from 15% to 20% with a premium of 30% or 40% to put the hotels that are prepared to pay at the top of the listings. Their market dominance could easily see many smaller hotels go out of business and the costs for larger hotels rise.

Some large hotel chains in America have already seen what could happen and are trying to fight back by creating their own online booking agents but it may be too late.

The second point is that by being market dominant these companies can start to influence the way people think. I have already talked about the Free Cancellation Policy and how quickly guests have come to think it is acceptable to book rooms to hold them then cancel them at short notice. There is talk in the mainstream media of the influence that Facebook might have had on the American elections. All around us the technology giants are dominating all aspects of our lives and with their very clever algorithms they can see inside people's lives, their behaviour and consequently tailor messages for their advertisers. Advertising used to be subliminal but there is no need anymore, it can be obvious because the technology companies know what their users like and can go to them directly. This impacts on the hotel and BnB industry. The OTAs are affecting guests' behaviour as already discussed, and we in the industry can only guess what the next set of subliminal or direct messages will be. What we can be assured of is that they will be for the benefit of the OTAs and not the hotels. Imagine if Booking.com in pursuit of higher profits bought a hotel chain, they could direct all enquiries through their website directly by having it at the top of the search engine. They could even manipulate the market to drive down the value of hotels to be able to buy it at the cheapest price. They could even ensure their rooms were at the most competitive because their hotel wouldn't have the same marketing costs as their competitors.

According to Global Justice Now, 69 of the top 100 economic entities are corporations or to phrase it another way, only 31 of the top 100 economic entities are countries. It's hard to imagine but that is the rate of change, in 2002 it was 49 countries and 51 corporations.

Now, Darwinism really is prevailing with the technology behemoths buying any potential threat to them. Often paying out insane amounts of money for loss making companies just to ensure their market dominance. In the past governments stopped this happening by legislation or breaking up all dominant monopolies but today they seem impotent or afraid to do anything about the behemoths that are genuinely striding across our planet with impunity.

Although Google, Facebook, Amazon, Apple, Baidu and Alibaba may be untouchable now, their power only comes from people using them. There may be a time when a cultural backlash changes that but now that seems impossible. These companies collectively can move public opinion and bring down governments and it is extraordinary how quickly this has happened. Imagine what they can do to a little BnB in Staffordshire.

Does this mean that we at Marlow House are on a crusade to bring these technology giants down? No, but we can do something to combat their dominance and try to regain some independence and safeguard our future. Many within the trade only see the rise of technology for good and an enhancement to their business but I believe they are being short sighted.

AirBnB

AirBnB is another extraordinary company that has grown so quickly and has truly been a disruptor. Giving property owners the opportunity through their platform to rent out a room or a sofa to raise some spare cash seemed like a brilliant idea of emancipation enabling the shared society to backlash against global corporatism, big hotel chains and profiteering. It gave the little man a chance to earn a little money on the side, the chance for impoverished travellers to seek out inexpensive digs and as part of the founder's altruism to bring like-minded people together over a bowl of beans and a glass of wine. It truly was a fantastic idea and caught the imagination. AirBnB just took off so naturally it wasn't long before corporate greed and the bigger financial opportunity diluted all the original ideas of group benefit and one planet.

AirBnB is a classic of unintended consequences. I have no doubt that the original founders Brian Chesky, Joe Gebbia and Nathan Blecharczyk wanted to give downtown San Franciscans the chance to make some cash and meet new people. Very quickly landlords around the world saw this as an opportunity to get more rent for their second homes and investments than by having long term tenants who also have rights that were hard fought for over time. As a result, overcrowded cities found themselves with a shortage of rental properties as landlords changed their business models in search of higher returns. Hotels found themselves unable to compete against a company that owns no hotels, offers accommodation that doesn't have to comply with any health and safety or compliance and that doesn't have to be registered for VAT. AirBnB as a global technology company can determine where its modus operandi lies for tax purposes so pays very little tax and can constantly reinvest, leading to uninhibited meteoric growth. A hotel chain with a five-year refurbishment plan could easily have found itself offside during that period as AirBnB stole significant market share.

It would be great to think that AirBnB just grew the size of the travelling market but that would be naive and the sort of thing their CEO or legal counsel would speculate in front of a Commons Select Committee. They have used their technology to take a significant slice out of the market by brokering a product that doesn't comply with modern legislation because it is ahead of Governments and compliance. Governments are finally catching up though and now at the time of writing landlords in London can only rent out up to 90 days per annum with AirBnB making that model unsustainable which should bring a lot of rentable property back into the marketplace for deserving Londoners who need somewhere to live. AirBnB is a global company disrupting markets globally and yet legislation to try and redress this disruption is having to be battled out piecemeal by individual cities and local governments. In the meantime, established businesses who pay their business rates, VAT and corporation tax as well as NIC and employees taxation see their market being challenged driving rates down as a result.

As consumers, we have all benefitted from these technologies, but we need to understand the end game which is simply illustrated here.

CHAPTER 8
TECHNOLOGY AND ITS IMPACT

We live ten miles from our nearest town in a sleepy hamlet. For years we have had to pay £22-£24 for a taxi to take us home after midnight from the town centre if we have enjoyed a night out.

A couple of years ago a very enterprising taxi company owner rented the Uber technology. This meant that we could acquire his App and order taxis through a mobile device. We could still do it the old-fashioned way as well by ringing his call centre. The taxi driver would get the order to come and collect us and his technology would bring him directly to our phone so no more getting lost on the way. The technology also allowed us to choose the type of vehicle, the make, model and even look at a profile of the driver. Each would show their proximity, time of arrival and the price they would charge.

Within a few months the price had dropped to £14 for the same journey. Clearly that is great news for us and all the other people using this service but just think about this for a moment.

The taxi driver must pay £150 every Monday in advance to the very clever man who bought the software. He now has 1000 taxis who use his software. Very quickly as this excellent piece of technology was available most people who have a requirement for a taxi adopted it because it is so efficient, so simple to use and gave them a great saving. It also consolidated the taxi industry making more taxis available so that the speed of getting a taxi improved. It really was a no-brainer for the user. After a while, taxi drivers had no choice but to join this man's taxi business meaning that there were now more drivers competing for the same work driving the price down. Other taxi companies then starting to go out of business giving this very clever man market dominance. Where does his profit come from? Having as many taxi drivers as possible paying £150 every Monday morning. He may be truly altruistic, but I think he is just counting the money every Monday and it is a lot of money.

The taxi drivers however have seen a standard fare of £22 drop to £14 and must pay £150 every Monday to get any bookings at all. I never met a wealthy taxi driver when we used to pay £22 and I wonder if I will ever meet one now the same journey is £14. Has the cost of petrol, insurance, servicing or buying a car also dropped by 40% during that time? This means that either the taxi driver must take a huge cut in income or will work longer and longer hours or cut corners on his outgoings like servicing and insurance.

This won’t happen overnight, logically many drivers will stop in favour of higher paid work elsewhere or in a different industry. This industry however isn't regulated like other parts of the taxi world which is why the black cab drivers and yellow cabs of New York have been taking Uber to court. It seems almost unbelievable that a business that was so full of legislation should come under pressure from a new pretender in the market that can operate with barely any legislation at all.

Just as the courts and Government try to catch up though, Uber which is unbelievably profitable (after all it has never bought a taxi, employed a driver, bought any new tyres or petrol) is throwing its enormous financial weight behind driverless cars. Uber understands that it has established a relationship with the user (you and I) and if it can get rid of the drivers and all that horrible legislation that they know will accompany them once the legal world catches up with them, then they will see their profits go stratospheric as the only cost will be the vehicle itself. Elon Musk and others are developing electric cars that may well be superseded by even more energy efficient modes of transportation. The vehicles could be owned by Uber, BMW, or The Norwich Union but the power will lie in the relationship between Uber and the user and that is what will be monetised. The result will be millions of taxi drivers globally made redundant as they will never be able to compete with the new business model and Uber will almost certainly cut them out anyway, after all, staff have rights and can be a bit needy, software and machines never talk back or complain, at least not yet.

Disruptive technology brings enormous short-term benefits to most of us but as they become dominant there are casualties. We must always remember that driving these businesses, once the original creators have taken their money and left, are corporations and people driven by profit. Some may have other more ominous agendas.

Historically those that control capital control everything, at least until the masses rise. Today those that control capital also control the power of communication which is a heady combination. On one hand they can use their technology to bring financial savings to many but only by squeezing the producers of goods and services. We all want to pay less for things, but we must accept that this cannot go on forever. We are finally having that discussion here in the UK about our National Health system. With more old people living longer and now another mini baby boom the pressures are enormous and yet the obvious thing which is for each of us to pay more seems to be far too difficult for us to discuss sensibly as a society. The problem is that the young and the old do not necessarily have the income but are the greatest users of the system, but we are asking those who are working and use it least to pay more.

We are all happy to have cheaper taxi fares but how do we feel about those taxi drivers whose income has fallen 40% and those that may lose their jobs altogether? Many might say, it's their problem, they will have to find something else to do, but the fact is that the technology revolution will affect us all. I am sure doctors and lawyers will be more vocal when algorithms take their jobs.

It's hard to imagine how a BnB could ever be taken over by technology. A weekend break away wouldn't really be the same if all the staff were robots so on the face of it, it seems quite a safe business to be in but as I have demonstrated, disruptive technology is having an impact on profitability. One way or another we are all going to be affected and it's no good ignoring it. I have spoken to a few friends who are involved in car dealerships and not one will accept even the possibility of the advent of driverless cars, they all say that it will never happen and even if it did people would still want to own their own car. These friends are of a certain age and don't realise that car ownership is not important to young people who regard travel as something that must be done, just another commodity. My generation, the baby boomers saw car ownership as a rite of passage and thereafter a reflection of social standing. Badge envy was our version of Facebook profile pictures. That is now truly an anachronism.

I have just had a situation recently where I needed a solicitor to do some conveyancing on a piece of land. I shopped around and found a fixed fee company who can do it all online for £528.00. My local solicitor, very old school and still living in the 1980s, quoted a basic cost of £2,400 plus £190 per hour and we all know how that can wrack up. Her figures reflect what she needs to run her Mercedes and send her children to private school because that is the way it has always been. Even some very bright people cannot see what is happening around them.

Disruptive Technology

"Disrupters don't have to discover something new; they just have to discover a practical use for new discoveries" - Jay Samit.

The BnB industry has been around for thousands of years

in one guise or another. Hotels are just large-scale BnBs with a few extra knobs and whistles. The industry has survived and thrived through many periods of change and innovation.

Cafe René in the sitcom *Allo Allo* had to walk the line between looking after his local French customers in Nouvion, France whilst maintaining relationships with the German occupiers and playing host to the French Resistance. This may have been a very clever script but isn't so far from the truth. When Joseph and Mary arrived without a confirmed booking in Bethlehem a quick-thinking proprietor came up with a solution. Small business operators have always been capable of being fleet of foot, today's challenges are just another one of those times. The threats posed by the online booking agencies may not seem as obvious as problems resulting from an occupying army or pestilence and plague but in their own way they are just as challenging; maybe more so.

The current technology revolution is happening so fast. Forbes suggests that the key to surviving is to "Accelerate your speed of execution as well as your ability to seize new opportunities." That is quite tricky as a hotel or BnB. Re-inventing yourself isn't that straightforward. Hotels have historically grown and thrived by return business. A business traveller or family holidaying will by choice return to a BnB that has looked after them and where they have been made to feel welcome. A good establishment will carry a premium which it may discount to returning guests akin to a loyalty bonus. Even that basic premise has been changed thanks to those very smart people at the OTAs (online travel agencies). As soon as I hear an acronym, any acronym, my hackles rise.

In this industry the market leaders are Expedia and Booking.com. Expedia dominate in the USA and Booking.com in Europe. To illustrate the rapid change in the market I will share a few facts about Booking.com. Started by Geert-Jan Bruinsman, a very clever Dutchman, in his bedroom in 1996, he saw an opportunity to help people looking for a room for the night by putting them in touch with hotels. Initially he couldn't even get *De Telegraaf*, the highest circulating newspaper in Holland to run an ad for him because they wouldn't accept an advert without a telephone number and he just wanted to give a web address. This reminds me of when Alexander Graham Bell approached William Orton of The Western Union in 1876 to pay for the patent for his invention, the telephone. Mr Orton dismissed it as nothing more than a toy even though Graham Bell suggested that "One day there will be a telephone in every major city." I doubt that the person in charge of advertising at *De Telegraaf* for Mr Bruinsman could have imagined Booking.com's reach and dominance within 20 years.

The size of the undertaking that Bruinsman and his colleagues embarked upon was breath-taking. Persuading hotels and BnBs to list with them when nothing like this existed before. It must have been very painful telephoning and visiting them one by one painting a vision to an industry that is quite cautious and had never really marketed itself; apart from the large chains.

Within a few years an American technology company that wasn't really going anywhere paid the founders $113m. That business has grown today with a market capitalisation of $81bn. Remember I said that two big players dominated the industry? The other being Expedia in America. Well, Expedia refused to buy Booking.com in 2002. Booking.com is today widely regarded as the best acquisition in internet history declaring a $1.1bn profit in 2011 alone. It now has 1,000,000 properties on its site and books over 900,000 room nights daily. It's share price has grown from $100 in 2009 to $1100 in 2016 and $1647 at the time of writing. In 2006 it had only 27,000 properties on its books and staffing of 85. Today it boasts 14,000 employees. This has all led the EU to warn that Booking.com and TripAdvisor may now have reached market dominance beyond the point of no return.

Expedia, who missed a golden opportunity, still command a market capitalisation of $17bn, mightily impressive but only a quarter of the value of Booking.com who last year developed a close working relationship to create a travel industry behemoth. Analysts and reporters will often talk about the dominance of the FAANGs - Facebook, Apple, Amazon, Netflix and Google - but quietly under the radar Booking.com and Tripadvisor have come to dominate the huge hotel industry.

CHAPTER 9
TRIPADVISOR REVIEWS

A classic situation where the balance of power is horrendously skewed is the online review websites. Guests can leave the most damning reviews for a whole host of reasons. There have been recorded instances of competitors leaving horrible reviews and the owners being unable to have them taken down. Fortunately, we have never had anything like that happen, overall our guests have been very generous with their time and their reviews. Many websites don't even allow the right to reply but fortunately TripAdvisor does. Below are a few less than generous reviews we have received over the last few years. We are always happy to receive constructive criticism. We acknowledge that we might become complacent over time, so a poor review is always a little livener to keep us on our toes. Having said that, a review that we feel is not a reflection of the guests' visit may well get a balanced but damning reply. Most BnB owners probably wouldn't be as direct but, in my view, we should have the right to reply and if guests feel they can say unpleasant things about us, particularly personal things then I see no reason to hold back. Fortunately, within the hotel industry there is a website on the dark web where all hotel owners can go to discuss guests in detail, leaving individual and personal reviews so that information can be shared to ensure difficult guests are either blackballed or get "preferential treatment" when staying. It is an opportunity for BnB owners to vent their frustration, it can be extraordinarily cathartic, and the owners can collectively laugh and share their stories and experiences. It's an amazing forum and it keeps all of us sane. Of course, it doesn't exist! Or does it?

Caroltwocoats from Bristol
Disappointing
Reviewed 9 June 2014
Marlow House is in a lovely part of the country with beautiful views. Unfortunately, our stay was spoiled by the inhospitable attitude of Jane. When we first arrived she seemed friendly enough, though her incessant questioning did become rather overbearing to the point that we felt we were being interrogated - it was supposed to be a relaxing break!
For some peculiar reason the following day we were blatantly ignored by her even when we wished her, "Good morning" at breakfast. She never spoke to us again! We felt unwelcome and were glad when it was time to leave.
Stayed January 2014, travelled as a couple

Reply: Steve H, Owner at Marlow House Bed & Breakfast, responded to this review:
Thank you, Caroltwocoats from Bristol for your review. Whilst we appreciate that all guests are free to voice their opinions we are somewhat bemused as to your review six months after your visit. Presumably you were so upset and disappointed it took you a good while to recover. Checking our guest list for January, we do not even have a Carol from Bristol who stayed although perhaps you were travelling incognito. Nevertheless, if you felt that Jane was overbearing and excessively inquisitive we apologise, we have been married for 25 years and I am constantly told by one and all just how lucky I am to have met the sweetest, kindest and most considerate person in the world. Your description does not resemble that person at all, so I can only assume that if you did indeed visit Marlow House that day (perhaps in disguise) then you met an alien who had descended upon earth and temporarily taken her place. Please look at the other 167 reviews for confirmation. I have had a quick look at your review history and damning reports seem to be your thing, it's good to have a hobby. If

we genuinely disappointed, then we are remorseful and apologetic but given that we are struggling to find out if you even stayed in January we cannot offer any more insight at this point. We try to make everyone who visits Marlow House as welcome and comfortable as possible. We offer our home up to our guests, welcoming everyone in almost as extended family which usually involves a little conversation.

We are very happy to take constructive criticism on the chin as it helps us to improve what we are offering however in this instance we feel your remarks are the complete converse of what all our other guests enjoy about staying at Marlow House. If indeed you did stay, then clearly, we were just not the right kind of establishment for you but fortunately there are plenty of vanilla death by boredom hotels throughout the UK to visit.

Jane and Steve

<u>Loved to have met the owners</u>
Reviewed 7 March 2016
We booked this BnB based on thinking the owners would help us explore the county, but they were away on hols themselves and Sharon the caretaker tried to be helpful but just didn't know enough. The accommodation was good, but we felt we missed out on some things
Stayed October 2015, travelled as a couple.

Reply: Steve W, Owner at Marlow House Bed & Breakfast, responded to this review:

Hi Toni and Marie. Thank you so much for leaving a review about your visit here in September of last year. Jane and I are sorry that we weren't here to meet you. It would have been our pleasure to have given you tips on where to go although we have so much information in our guest lounge, we are really surprised that our lovely lady Sharon did not point you in the direction of all the local information that is there. Should you return to England in the future please give us notice so that we can re-arrange our holidays to be here to act as your tour guides, we are both really mortified that your stay was not as perfect as it could have been because we chose to take a holiday at that time and left you to manage your own itinerary. We appreciate that guests like the owners to be here all the time which has led us to re-consider our holiday plans in the future. Thank you for making us aware of our shortcomings, we have a business to run and should be more thoughtful and diligent for our guests needs.

Jane and Steve

<u>disappointed</u>
Reviewed 18 September 2014
The hotel was lovely with fab gardens and fab views. BUT our bedroom was not clean and the toilet was so close to the shower you could use both at the same time. Breakfast was not good sausages and bacon and even the bread was not good to taste. The lady in the kitchen dropped a sausage so the next couple only got one and a half sausage each, and for £90 pound a night this was not good. They only take cash payment but when I asked for a receipt for our two night stay was told they don't gave receipts, so you have no proof you have paid. Will not be going back to this hotel...
Stayed September 2014, travelled as a couple

Reply: Steve W, Owner at Marlow House Bed & Breakfast, responded to this review
Hi Robert. Thank you for your review. We are pleased that you thought the house and gardens were fab. We were very sorry to hear that you had some complaints about your stay. This was the first time that Jane and I had gone away and left the BnB in the hands of one of our helpers so naturally we were mortified to hear that you were disappointed with your stay. Looking back at the 232 previous reviews you can see that we strive to do the very best we can.
With regards to the toilet being too close to the shower this is not something that has ever been commented on

before. Nobody has ever complained or even mentioned this, but we take on board your remarks although it may be difficult for us to reconfigure the bathroom based on your comment.

We were shocked to hear that the bedroom was not clean. We left to go on our holiday the day you arrived. We acknowledge that there were guests in the room the previous evening. We have very strict guidelines for our cleaners, so we will be taking this up with them, this has come as a complete shock to us as we have never had an issue with cleanliness.

We do find it surprising that if our member of staff did drop a sausage then she would have surely cooked another but fortunately it wasn't yourselves that were deprived of half a sausage but another guest who to date has not complained. About the taste of the food, taste is very subjective. We source all our products carefully, our sausages and bacon come from a local pig farm that supply a number of the UK's most well-known restaurants. Reading back over the previous 50 or so reviews I couldn't help but notice how many other people had remarked specifically how good our breakfasts are. As I said, the taste of food is quite an individual thing and naturally we bow to your preferences but on the whole we have found our breakfasts to be hugely popular and we have told many guests at their request where our bread comes from because many find it so tasty we are just sorry that these were not to your tastes.

With regard to your invoice, we have been home for three hours and have just sent you an email to see if you would like it emailed or a hard copy posted. An invoice is not a problem at all, the lady who looked after you does not use our computers so was unable to raise one while you were here. It is possible that when she told you she couldn't give you an invoice at the time she may have explained it in a way that implied we do not give receipts or invoices which or course is not the case.

Jane and I are both so sorry that your stay did not meet your expectation. This is such a rarity as I am sure you can appreciate having seen all the previous reviews. Our lady who kindly stepped in, in our absence is an extremely hard working and conscientious person who did her best. Other guests remarked how lovely she was and it is just a pity that for your visit the standards were not as we strive for.

Jane and Steve

Excellent location...shame about the owner

Reviewed 2 June 2014 via mobile

I booked Marlow House for my family who were staying there and when we first arrived we were blown away by the location and the rooms. You literally can't get better I imagine. The only thing that let it down for all of us was how useless Steve the owner was. His inability to be flexible, his complaining over insignificant issues made it difficult at times. His wife unfortunately wasn't there at the weekend and as I understand it she usually runs the rental side of the business which was unfortunate as I felt that Steve was out of his depth on his own and added stress to what is an already stressful situation.

Reply: Steve W, Owner at Marlow House Bed & Breakfast, responded to this review

Hi Alan and Mia. Firstly, we hope you had a lovely wedding. Given how poor the weather had been that week, it really came good on the day. When Jane and I first read your review, we thought you were joking. Perhaps you were not aware of everything that was going on as you were staying out of the way of the bride. (In point of fact you were not even meant to be there that morning). You booked the house for 11 people. Mia said she would like breakfast for all the guests for 9am. The first guests arrived at 7.45 because there had been no communication. Not a problem at all. Everyone was sat down by 8 and breakfasts were being prepared. By 9.30 I had cooked a variety of breakfast for 19 people. Cars were pulling up left right and centre and in the end the drive was completely full and I was directing vehicles to park at the back of the house. In all there were 23 people in the house. There were people turning up requesting towels so that they could shower even though they were not paying guests here.

I may have seemed a little flustered, and you are correct I was on my own, because managing 11 is not really an issue but double that made it considerably more difficult. If I had been told the night before I could have put extensions on the table and had everything prepared, as it was I was reacting to a constantly changing situation. I said nothing on the day because it was your wedding day and didn't want to say anything that might have spoilt it. I spoke to your father the next day because one of the rooms remained unpaid at that time and I asked for a small contribution to all the extra breakfasts and laundry which he paid promptly without any discussion.

Quite frankly I am staggered as I was expecting an email to say how we had gone the extra mile under very difficult circumstances. On the Monday morning your Mum and Grandma seemed mortified that we had been put through so much extra work and even said themselves that they had no idea who all the people were coming to the house. I had two lots of guests request details because they wanted to return. I suppose everything in life is perspective, clearly you felt that I was out of my depth whilst I thought the organisation of your party was shambolic with nobody having the faintest idea who anyone was or what was going on. I suppose we will have to beg to differ.

Jane and Steve

Very comfortable B & B

Reviewed 17 October 2016 via mobile.

My wife and I stayed at Marlow House for two nights in September. On arrival we were shown to our room by Josh who looked after us very well throughout our stay. Our room at the front was spacious and the view was beautiful.

We had booked dinner for the first night and the cream tea for the second day. The dinner cooked by Josh was excellent and ample portions. The same was true of the breakfasts.

My two issues are the steep nature of the stairs, difficult to negotiate for the older person (like us) but I obviously accept that, short of a major reconstruction, little can be done. But perhaps worth making the point in the literature.

My other concern was the size of the cream tea. I am afraid that I do not consider a cream tea to consist of just one scone, albeit with plenty of cream and jam, and one slice of fruit cake.

That apart, we enjoyed our stay.

Stayed September 2016, travelled as a couple

Reply: Steve W, Owner at Marlow House Bed & Breakfast, responded to this review

Dear John. Thank you for taking the time to leave a review. We are so pleased to hear that you had a good time. Jane and I are sorry we weren't here to look after you both, but it sounds as though Josh looked after you very well.

We were sorry to hear that you felt the stairs were steep. They are in fact the same as almost all stairs in the UK, they travel for 10" (the tread) and rise for 8" (the rise). Despite being 176 years old they comply exactly with the current Government recommendations.

We do have more steps than a standard house. Marlow House is early Victorian and one of its lovely features is the high ceilings. Higher ceilings on the ground floor inevitably means more steps to get up to the first floor. As a result, we have 16 steps as opposed to the normal 13 steps in a modern house with lower ceilings. The additional 3 steps therefore may be quite illusory giving the impression of a much more substantial staircase.

We are aware that we have more stairs than a modern house and these are illustrated in the images 30 and 32 in the picture gallery on our website.

In the past we have taken phone and email enquiries from elderly and infirm guests asking about stairs and access because they are acutely aware of their own requirements. It would be imprudent and overzealous for us to ask everyone who enquires about staying if they are in any way incapacitated or if their movement is diminished but perhaps we should in the future. For those that struggle with stairs we always suggest taking our Coach House which is on the ground floor and obviates the need for stairs completely. Most guests who are staircase challenged tend to book the Coach House.

On our next changes to the website we will make further mentions that we have three extra steps to climb. Jane and I hope that it wasn't too burdensome for you and did not spoil your stay. We have considered major reconstruction to address this issue as you intimated but generally our guests enjoy the space and light that the high ceilings offer. Removing three feet from the entire middle of the house we feel would detract from some of the charm here at Marlow House.

We are so pleased that you found the breakfasts and dinner with Josh to be excellent and with ample portions but naturally were disappointed to hear that you felt the cream tea to be unsatisfactory regarding size. With over 3000 guests in the almost 4 years that we have been open we have never had a comment suggesting that our food was insufficient. Perhaps you felt there wasn't enough variety and we have taken this on board. We encourage all our guests to ask for more if they are still hungry, perhaps Josh did not do this, but we would have hoped that during your stay you would have felt comfortable asking for something else to satisfy your appetite.

Should you decided to visit Marlow House again in the future we will make a point of providing you with a cream tea that will remain in your memory in perpetuity.

Once again, despite a few issues that you have kindly brought to our attention for our own improvement we are so pleased that you enjoyed your stay and hope that we can meet you personally in the future.

Jane and Steve

A lovely stay

Reviewed 21 July 2016 via mobile

Stayed here for a weekend for my boyfriend's birthday with our friends. We stayed in the Coach House which was a 2 story annexe to the main house. There were 2 single beds which were quickly pushed together by Steve for our stay and a large bed upstairs with a sitting area, sofa and TV. This was an ideal set up for relaxing together.

Breakfast was plentiful and varied and the conservatory views were stunning. Afternoon tea was lavish. Molly the dog and Abbey the cat added a sense of home to our stay.

Access to the nearby town was made exceptionally easy with directions on a printed sheet and lunch venues were helpfully recommended.

Steve and Jane were both very helpful with our reservation and were attentive to our needs through our stay.

Thank you for a lovely stay.

Stayed July 2016, travelled as a couple

Reply: Steve W, Owner at Marlow House Bed & Breakfast, responded to this review:

Hi Amy. Thank you so much for taking the time to leave such a positive review, it does sound as though you had an amazing time here. It would be lovely from our own personal and business development to know what was lacking to not get a full 5* review as your very kind and lengthy overview implies everything was spot on.

Hopefully you will find an opportunity to return, it would be a pleasure to see you all again

Jane and Steve

Night before marriage

Reviewed 18 August 2015 via mobile

We visited Saturday just gone for my wedding on the Sunday. Steve showed us to our room and grabbed us some beers, he explained the bits and bobs we needed to know and they went out for the night. We stayed in a large room/mini house basically 2 singles down and a double upstairs. It was a really good setting for a few beers in the sofa area upstairs then we headed out for some food. The next morning, we had breakfast which was cooked by Jane, we had fresh fruit and everything you would expect from a cooked breakfast, the sausage was right up there in quality, the bacon was the opposite but each to their own, no big deal at all. Jane encouraged us to play our own music on the docking station. The one small detail that impressed me most was we had already paid, already eaten breakfast and when Steve asked would we like anymore food I declined, he went on to explain that I had a long day ahead and wouldn't be eating for a while, me saying yes would have created more work (cooking) for him. That stood out for me as impressive. In all fairness there isn't much more that could have been done to gain a 5/5

The pets give a real homely feel and the owners seem like great people. I appreciate you making us feel welcome. If you are getting married at the castle there is no risk, book here. There is one minor detail. Get a bigger sign indicating you are Marlow House.

Stayed August 2015, travelled with friends

Reply: Steve W, Owner at Marlow House Bed & Breakfast, responded to this review

Thank you for your lovely review. Hopefully the wedding went well. We always try to look after our guests as best we can especially if they are getting married. Glad you enjoyed the beers, just our little gift to help you enjoy the evening before the big day.

We are so pleased you appreciated the extra effort we put in to make sure you and the rest of your wedding group had a relaxing stay.

Of course it is a shame that you didn't like the bacon, food taste is very subjective. Our butcher has won many awards

and supplies some of the finest restaurants in the country but even so we do not rest on our laurels. Every year Jane and I do a taste test at our local food Festival of more than ten suppliers of sausages and bacon to ensure that we are getting what we think is the best that we can buy from our local suppliers. We do know that some people find that our food has a different taste to what you buy in the supermarkets because our locally produced food is not processed in anyway, it is a critical part of our sourcing policy. If you choose to visit us again we will make a point of picking up a pack of bacon from the supermarket so that you have a choice.
Unfortunately there isn't much I can do about the sign, it is already five feet wide and 18" tall and is set into the sandstone wall at the bottom of the drive next to the entrance gates. I can appreciate that you might have had a lot on your mind with the wedding and could have missed it.
We do email all of our guests before they arrive with accurate directions and ask that they ignore their satnavs because many of them take you off in a different direction.
Jane and I are so pleased that you had a great time here and hope that you come and visit us again soon, perhaps for a wedding anniversary

Jane and Steve

<u>Would love to return if on special offer again!</u>
Reviewed 26 October 2014
Wonderful place, wonderful host and hostess and excellent food! Didn't know it was such an interesting historic town! Lots to do and the location of Marlow House is gorgeous! Highly recommend it!

Reply: Steve W, Owner at Marlow House Bed & Breakfast, responded to this review:
We are so pleased that you enjoyed your stay and discovered that our town and Staffordshire generally is a wonderful county. Naturally we are a little disappointed

that you felt we need to be on special offer to make a return visit, the plethora of special offers that awash our industry bely the fact that as the owners of the business we work extremely hard to offer a memorable experience. Owners of BnBs can only dream of earning the minimum wage but we do understand that there is so much choice out there. Fortunately, we now have so many guests making return visits having experienced all we have to offer at Marlow House, we hope that you can appreciate everything that goes into making the experience you so clearly enjoyed, and you will one day return on its own merits.

Jane and Steve

Reviewed 12 May 2017 via mobile

Terrible service

Booked a hotel room months ago, then received a lousy text message saying they had to cancel my booking due to unavoidable circumstances. They then suggested they could help relocate me and would include me in emails but still not received anything, nor did I receive any information for other hotels despite being promised many times.

I have obviously looked into other hotels but all of the local ones to the wedding venue were fully booked months before I made the initial booking. When I checked their website it said that two bookings were made within the last few days? I'm not sure why they didn't want my booking but this is unacceptable and they should apologise for how they have ruined my weekend where I was supposed to attend my friend's wedding.

Do not book with this hotel! They do not know what customer service is and obviously don't care.

Reply: Steve W, Owner at Marlow House Bed & Breakfast, responded to this review Responded 17 May 2017

Dear Mr Singh. Thank you for taking the time to leave such a lengthy and damning review especially in the light of the fact that you didn't even stay here. I am very pleased that TripAdvisor gives us the opportunity to reply. I was in two minds whether to take the time to reply or not but given this is the worst review we have had in the four years we have been trading I felt I ought to just to enlighten anyone looking at this as to the true facts of the matter.

You contacted us on the 18th February to book a room for Saturday 27th May for two people for one night. You gave me your email address and I sent you a confirmation (and a request for a deposit, which was never paid) on the email address that you gave me.

On the 8th March I emailed you and text you to inform you that due to circumstances beyond our control we would have to cancel your reservation. We were very apologetic as it is not normally something that we do. I offered to send you a list of hotels in our area and duly did so on the same day. I thought that almost 12 weeks' notice would be sufficient time for you to find other accommodation.

On the 19th of April (some six weeks later) you sent me a text which read:

Steve. I have still not received any emails from any alternative hotels after you cancelled my booking for the 27th May. Can you let me know who best to contact as places are booked up now. Mr Singh.

Had you thought that I would contact hotels on your behalf and ask them to email you?

I noticed that you had left it six weeks before trying to find alternative accommodation.

I then asked you to send me your email address again (because naturally I thought you would have found something else by now) which you duly did and I sent you a list of hotels on the 20th April (the following day).

I next received a text from you on Friday 12th of May some three weeks later (whilst I was on holiday abroad). It read:

Steve. I still haven't received a list of hotels from you.

I replied immediately and asked if you had checked your

SPAM as I had sent it to you twice on 8th March and 20th April. You said you had so I then texted back to you a lengthy list of hotels in the area close to Marlow House. I then emailed a few friends who have hotels and continued to text you for the next hour trying to help you resolve your problem. I was doing all of this from my hotel room in another country whilst our friends waited patiently for me. I continued to mail you and eventually two days later you replied saying: No help needed I have made other arrangements.

I agree that it was not ideal that we had to cancel your original booking but I do feel we have some prerogative to be able to do this and we did give you 12 weeks' notice. You then point out that on our website it said two bookings were made in the last few days. This wasn't on our website but on Booking.com's website who use all kinds of tools to encourage bookings, the day we informed you, we immediately blocked out all the rooms, there were no rooms available as soon as I had contacted you.

Jane and I do our very best to help all of our guests and potential guests and this is reflected in the 500+ reviews we have here on TripAdvisor. In this instance we did everything we could to try and find you alternative accommodation. I notice that your moniker on TripAdvisor is spelt amssingh with 2 x the letter S rather than the 1 x letter S you gave me with your email address. That might explain why you said you hadn't received my emails with hotel lists. I do feel that your difficulties in finding accommodation have more to do with leaving things too late given that it is a Bank Holiday weekend, the initial gap of 6 weeks before contacting me and then the subsequent three weeks before contacting me again.

You informed me on Sunday that you have now found alternative accommodation and are attending your friend's wedding on Saturday so I am not entirely sure how your weekend has been ruined as you are now attending your friend's wedding. In conclusion as far as I can see you

were mildly inconvenienced by our cancelling your room giving you 12 weeks' notice to find another room but you chose to do nothing about it and when it got very late and there wasn't much availability it was easier for you to blame me than accept that perhaps you should have taken a more proactive approach.
If I wasn't so busy I would consider applying to be your personal concierge but I am not sure we would work very well together.
Just so that you know, your damning (and in my view wholly incorrect and unjustified) review means that the TripAdvisor algorithms can no longer entertain us to enter their 20 Best BnB lists. It takes years to get to the position to even be considered but your one moment of getting something off your chest has done irretrievable damage to us. This is the inequality of online reviews, there is nothing I can to do inconvenience you at all (not that I would want to) and yet your inability to organise your own life has led us to be damned. I hope that anybody reading this will be able to take an objective view on what can only be described as a truly sorry affair.

Reviewed 6 October 2015
Disappointing !
Interesting venue in a beautiful setting but even more interesting that the loft room we were allocated is not promoted on the website. No wifi, no shower pressure (works if you run the sink but was damned cold), no locks on the door(!) and lethal beams running alongside the bed. The door jammed requiring such force to open it that you were in danger of hitting the aforementioned beams.
The informality of the hosts was refreshing, and the resident dog and cat were very affectionate companions but must say that I felt that overall the room was unsatisfactory and I did not enjoy my stay.... Even more disappointing given the overall standard of reviews from guests allocated the 'proper' room

Reply: Steve W, Owner at Marlow House Bed & Breakfast,

responded to this review Responded 7 October 2015
Thank you for your review. Jane and I are absolutely mortified to hear that you did not enjoy your stay with us, we can't understand why you didn't say something at the time if you were not happy, we would have done everything we could to have made your stay more compatible with your needs.
Unfortunately we were completely full that evening as you were attending a wedding along with your other friends (who also left a damning review) which is why you were in the upper part of the house. The family had allocated the rooms on your behalf, it was a pity that they were not fully aware of your exacting needs. I think it might have been better for all of us if you had stayed somewhere else.
The height of the rooms is restricted at the sides, we acknowledge that. I think that lethal is a bit strong as the beams are inanimate and hardly likely to leap out at you. I do not know why the water was cold, I really wish you had mentioned it. I have just been up to check the door and it opens perfectly well, perhaps something had jammed in it while you were there.
We acknowledge that the wifi is not great on the top floor, this is a very large house and despite all our boosters sometimes the signal can drop out.
Jane and I do our very best to meet the exacting standards of all of our guests, we have clearly fallen short on this occasion and for that we apologise.
It is a great shame that you and your friends had such a disappointing time at Marlow House when we have had nothing but high praise from the rest of the wedding group while they were here, the previous night and at the same time.

Jane and Steve

Reviewed 18 September 2015
<u>Not impressed</u>
I know I am going against the majority opinion and obviously I can

only comment on the room we were allocated and the service we received:
• the bed had solid wooden bits sticking out at 45 degrees at the ends and it was very easy to knock your legs on them (see picture 1 in Room/Suite album)
• the bathroom fittings were pretentious with a rectangular white ceramic basin looking like a 1950s kitchen (see picture 1 in Bathroom album), the shower with square controls had nowhere to put soap etc so you had to pick it up from the floor all the time and the space between the shower and the wall next to the loo was miniscule (fortunately we are both reasonably slim)
• we went to breakfast at about 9am and there were 6 people there already with the result that we waited for 35-40 minutes for our cooked breakfast order to be taken.
I would probably rate the place as average but, given the high price, I have downrated it to poor.

Reply: Steve W, Owner at Marlow House Bed & Breakfast, responded to this review Responded 19 September 2015
Thank you for taking the time to leave a review. Naturally we are sorry to hear that you did not enjoy your stay at Marlow House and had plenty of things to complain about. We were anticipating your review as we could tell you were unhappy while you were here. If it's any consolation your disappointment about Marlow House and the service and everything else it seems is entirely mutual.
We were very busy whilst you were here and it is true that you had to wait a while for your breakfast. Because we dine *en famille*, guests usually chat, enjoy their coffee, tea and cereal, taking in the views whilst they wait for a freshly cooked breakfast. Clearly you both enjoy your own company and chose not to engage with any of the other guests even though you had all attended the same wedding the previous evening and that of course is your prerogative.
With regard to your room and the decor, this is subjective.

We are sorry to hear that you found it pretentious. We were featured in 25 Beautiful Homes Magazine last year which in itself may also be pretentious. As you point out in your first line you are going against the grain which again is fine, we are all different, it would be less interesting if we were all the same.

Jane and I understand that we cannot please everyone we are just so disappointed that you did not have an enjoyable stay. When we heard you say, "I hate that dog", we knew that we probably wouldn't be able to turn things around. Molly also apologises for clearly being so horrible.

I think we will have to agree that our worlds do not cross over and it is probably best that if you visit the area again you choose to stay somewhere more suitable for your tastes and needs.

We will put our thinking hats on to see if there is anywhere we can recommend for you in the future should you wish to visit this beautiful area again but we may struggle.

Jane and Steve

CHAPTER 10
PUBLIC SECTOR RETIREES

We get many different people from all occupations and all ages. We have had pop starlets, TV presenters and producers, taxi drivers, builders, business people but by far the biggest group of guests we have are public sector workers and in particular public-sector retirees.

What many of them have in common is an extraordinary sense of entitlement. This is very pronounced and does not exist with any of our other guests. We accept that many of them have worked hard and done their term. We are often shocked how young many of them are and retired. We have had many police officers, detectives and firemen in their early fifties enjoying the fruits of their labour. They will all arrive in their new car paid for from their lump sum and then discuss their next cruise at the breakfast table.

My view is good luck to them, they entered a profession where the rewards were laid out and they are now benefitting from them. My concern is their disconnect from the rest of society and what is happening around them. The world is changing, and the UK is not immune. There are very few secure jobs today and hardly any that have the attractive pensions that the retirees who stay with us enjoy. For most public-sector workers, there is no paid-up pension pot, their future income is dependent on tomorrow's tax revenue but from what I hear they just do not grasp that. They have worked, they were promised and by God they are going to get it, after all, they have just booked the holiday to Cuba and the cruise around the Galapagos.

It wasn't that long ago that this would have been

considered a millionaires lifestyle, weekends away at posh BnBs in the countryside, dinners out every night in pubs and restaurants, theatre, holidays nonstop leapfrogging from one adventure to another with an intermittent bit of babysitting for grandchildren.

The papers are full of stories of this generation spending the inheritance but from what we have seen that isn't quite as it is. Almost without exception those arriving in a brand new little car and talking endlessly about their fantastic holidays are retired public sector workers. The self-employed and those still working understand how difficult life is and talk about the youngsters and their difficulties. The retired public-sector workers seem to be completely disconnected basking in their own good fortune. I am not blaming them or suggesting for a minute that they shouldn't enjoy what they were promised but it is clear to us seeing this every week that there is a massive imbalance.

The other thing that has been very noticeable is how many of them have been saying they took early redundancy. "They offered me early redundancy. I had to take it, I didn't want to keep working there, the pressure was too much." Everyone from the medical and teaching professions say this. From the way they talk, their pension shortfalls were made up making it a compelling reason to retire early, many of these were still in their early to mid-fifties at a time when most employed people in the private sector must work until they are 67 and the self-employed even longer.

It seems strange that as the demographic time bomb has exploded alongside a slowing growth in productivity a whole section of society is benefitting in a disproportionate way. It isn't as though they are a little bit better off, from what we can see, they are retiring ten to fifteen years before anyone else and are genuinely enjoying a lifestyle that would have been considered the preserve of the rich only twenty-five years ago.

Please be assured this isn't sour grapes or jealousy. I worked as an analyst for six years at Europe's oldest hedge fund. I understand the economics and how modern societies work and this is clearly wrong. My real interest whilst doing this work though was in sociology economics and human behaviour. This is the point that I am trying to make, probably very badly. This group just don't see how fortunate they are, they are unable to rationalise their circumstances in the context of today's society. The imbalance is massive and wholly disproportionate. Those who did enjoy a millionaire's lifestyle twenty-five years ago could only have done so from entrepreneurship unless they had some hugely desirable skill. Those entrepreneurs would have had to develop a product, create a marketplace, gone to market, employed people, taken risks, borrowed money and for the lucky ones, after a lot of work and worry along the way, it will have come good. They will have been able to retire in many cases exhausted and with less than perfect health to a millionaire's retirement of a new car, holidays in the sun, meals out and weekends away.

Today's public-sector retirees never had to take a risk, create a marketplace, or hope they got paid. They never had bad debts, banks on their back or worries about their business going bankrupt. They were guaranteed paid holidays, flexitime, sick pay, and critically very generous index linked pensions.

Even successful business people who retired in the last few years are not as well off as many public-sector employees who enjoy very generous pensions. It is much more likely that entrepreneurs retired by selling their business and banking some cash from which they now need to draw an income. With annuities as low as three percent they might need to have two million pounds in their kitty to enjoy the same annual income as many of our couples who come and stay with us. We are often amazed how many of our couples were both public sector workers, a medic and a teacher, a policeman and a social worker.

We have had retired hospital consultants to stay with us who were part of that last bastion who knew how to play the system before many of the loopholes were closed. Not content with earning a six figure sum plus private work that was only possible because they could use all the NHS facilities, in their last two years and this was common practice, they would stop all their private work and drive all their patients through the NHS, taking on as many lists as possible working seven days a week because their pension was predicated on the average earnings of their last two years in employment. This meant that many consultants took home a lump sum of five hundred thousand and an index linked pension of one hundred and seventy thousand pounds a year.

Until a couple of years ago some teachers were able to get promoted to a much higher grade for their last two years under the same scheme so that their pension reflected their average salary of the last two years. The same applied in the armed forces. It was a constant 'job for the boys', perpetuated to ensure that as many as possible got it. This happened because those making the rules knew that in time they would be benefitting from those rules.

A lot of this has ended now, thank goodness, but tomorrow's taxpayers, the youngsters of today will be paying for it over the next forty years. Quite why we are asking the workers of today to pay more tax when the retirees are enjoying incomes that bear no connection with today's circumstances is beyond me.

I shouldn't really be saying this as we are today's workers and we are reliant in many respects on this very affluent tranche of society. I just find myself biting my lip as they sit at our breakfast table with their very expensive pots of tablets and potions from the NHS regaling their next cruise around Norway and the highlights of the last musical they saw in London, New York, or Sydney. They are very nice people, but it would be lovely if they looked around and put their lives in context and thought about the youngsters.

The problem for society is that this group is very substantial, enough to swing an election. They will only ever vote for a party that maintains the status quo which will potentially skew elections for years to come.

CHAPTER 11
MEN OF A CERTAIN AGE

I constantly pigeon hole guests, I can't help it, it's just human nature. I have a very special group of guests that I call "men of a certain age".

This group is usually over the age of fifty although the majority tend to be over 60. They are nearly always men, in fact I can't think of an instance where they haven't been men and the majority are retired. How to describe them?

Let's start with a few examples. I have mentioned elsewhere in the book how I like to serve breakfasts piping hot on hot plates, it's just my thing, I enjoy food much more when it is hot and a whole lot less when it is cold. When we cook for friends, if I am cooking I insist on everyone starting even if I haven't had a chance to sit down at the table yet. I know it is polite to wait for everyone, especially the host and cook but I would much rather everyone enjoyed the benefit of my efforts rather than waiting and it is going cold and not getting what I consider to be the full experience; it's just my thing.

I like to make sure that all the meals served to our guests are piping hot. Sometimes the plates are very hot. I bring them to the table with oven gloves on and gingerly lay them down in front of guests with the jovial warning, "The plates are very hot, almost certainly beyond inquisitive hot, please don't touch them as I am too busy to take anyone to casualty". This invariably gets a little chuckle from around the table.

Now, perhaps I haven't been clear enough, perhaps I should have come to the table in an asbestos suit and red lights should have been flashing, perhaps we should have a paramedic stood at the end of the table with a defibrillator and some gauze, I completely understand that I may not have given enough warning. In fairness almost everybody acknowledges what I have said and as I turn their plate around so that it looks as appetising as possible almost everyone is happy to enjoy their lovely hot food except for one small group of guests, "men of a certain age".

I have in my past been a teacher and never had a problem telling a student that they shouldn't do something but it just doesn't seem appropriate to tell a fee-paying guest, a gentleman, almost certainly a retired Public Sector worker on an excellent pension enjoying life to the full, in his sixties, that he really shouldn't touch the plate.

"Steve told you not to touch the plate," his wife says out loud as he reels in pain having either grabbed the plate with both hands to turn it clockwise through ninety degrees because that is what he always does or because he has had to touch it, because that's what men of a certain age do.

I wish I could say that this has only happened a couple of times but it has happened dozens of times and always but always by a "man of a certain age". Unbelievably and I still find this hard to credit, we had a lovely family from South Wales staying who were utterly delightful but the father in his seventies did the same thing two days running much to the amusement of his family. I can only imagine that his fingers were screaming out to his brain to listen and learn.

It is a strange affliction that is never spoken about by all the analysts and commentators who try to create a new malaise and affliction for our society on a weekly basis. I don't think it can be diagnosed as a medical condition and it certainly can't be treated. But MOCA (because everything in this modern world has to be abbreviated and have an acronym - I think it's the law), is a very real affliction.

There have been a number of times during our five years of running the BnB where our house alarm has gone off during the night for no apparent reason. We wake up with a jolt in a semi trance of disturbed sleep to find the house in darkness and the electricity off. Immediately everything comes into sharp relief as the rota of guests goes through my mind as I dress and head off downstairs to the fuse board where the master for the alarm is. All this takes a few minutes by which time some guests have emerged to wonder what is going on. I reset the alarm and trip the fuse board so we have power and apologise to those inquisitive guests for the inconvenience. Heading back to bed I have already pinpointed the problem.

The following morning I expect one of the guests to come to me with a little admission but generally it doesn't happen. The "man of a certain age" skips over the issue, as does his wife, hoping that nobody noticed that during the night, he got up to go to the loo, listen to the shipping forecasts or England's second innings in Mumbai and knocked over the bedside lamp tripping all the electricity and setting off the alarm. If only this had been a one-off event but sadly not, it has happened on several occasions and most of the time we have been able to make a simple repair. But on two occasions the lamp was completely broken as it had been knocked onto the floor. They are always in pairs and sometimes we can't get a matching pair, so we must buy two new lamps at a cost of £160. On both of those occasions I could see where the "man of a certain age" had tried to mend the lamp, messed it up and then hoped we wouldn't notice. We have never chased guests for these damages, it happens very rarely, I just wish that these gentlemen would just leave it alone, tell me and then perhaps I can mend it before they destroy it with their tinkering.

Tinkering is the calling card of "men of a certain age". If they feel something isn't hanging straight, something doesn't sit squarely or doesn't look right, there is an overwhelming compunction for them to do something about it. I can almost hear their wives telling them to leave it alone, but they just can't help it. It's far worse than any addiction, it is utterly overwhelming. I am sure hardened heroin addicts have more resistance. This need for tinkering almost always ends up with something getting broken. Some will come and tell me, some will even admit what they have done but the majority just leave with the damaged article carefully propped up by a piece of cardboard at a jaunty angle to give them enough time to get down the drive.

We regard this as an occupational hazard and are now very alert upon the arrival of “men of a certain age”. In the great Venn diagram of life, the MOCA also cross over with the older age group in one area of causing damage; that of stair spindles. For those of you who are not familiar with the construction and benefits of staircases let me enlighten you. The newel posts, the big heavy upright posts top and bottom of a staircase when fitted properly carry the strength of the supporting rail known as the bannister. This is what you put your hand on and if required utilise to assist ascending the stairs. The 'Spindles' or decorative uprights that are underneath the bannister or handrail and there to create a barrier so that children don't easily fall through and to make it look pretty. They are only held in place by glue or pins because they are not designed to haul yourself up the staircase by. Unfortunately, MOCAs and more elderly gentlemen don't really appreciate this. I am forever repairing spindles. I do wonder how their own houses must look, I can only imagine that they are battered and bruised beyond belief, a war zone of accidental damage. Their wives must give a sigh of resignation as they see the spindle come away in the hand of their beloved MOCA. No one ever tells us when they have pulled a piece of our staircase apart.

Reprogramming the television is not the sole preserve of the MOCA, this tends to happen more often when children stay. But all too often a MOCA will for some inexplicable reason decide to manoeuvre a television, often pulling the aerial cable out (we have had some MOCAs actually dismantle the aerial cable leaving all the bits there). Reprogramming seems to be common. Most of our TVs have 150 channels but one can only assume that this isn't enough, the lack of 'Cabinet making' on channel 279 and 'brewing your own' on 347 is clearly spoiling his stay. We always know when he has tried to reprogram because the next guests tell us they can't get any channels. I have now learnt and always check the television when a MOCA checks out just as I check anything with moving parts, all joints on the furniture, hooks on the curtain tiebacks, in fact anything that can be fiddled with, tinkered with or generally altered.

We once knew a chap who had some kind of Asperger's or similar and whenever he stayed somewhere he had to re-arrange the furniture in a way that suited him better. I could cope with this if it was rearranged carefully.

When we started the bed and breakfast, a good friend of mine said that I should keep a diary of all the crazy goings on but surprisingly we haven't really had any ...

CHAPTER 12
GUEST STORIES

One might well say that mankind is divisible into two great classes: hosts and guests Max Beerbohm

Hospitality is making your guests feel at home, even if you wish they were. Anon

Trout Lips

One Friday with the BnB completely booked out for the weekend most of the guests had arrived and were settled in. They had returned from pubs and restaurants and were in their rooms, their cars all neatly parked up outside. At about 10pm a car pulled into the drive and parked right in the middle of the car parking area so that nobody could possibly move their cars without having to ask who's the Maserati was. It was the latest four doors and could not have been parked more obviously in the way.

The family that alighted was a mother and father in their late forties and a daughter aged about 11 or 12. They came in huffing and puffing about the journey up from Sussex and retired to their rooms.

The following morning the daughter came through to the kitchen about 7.30 to watch us make breakfast and talk at us pretty much non-stop. We quickly ascertained that she really wasn't getting much attention from her parents. We had our usual problem that the parents hadn't told us if she had any special dietary needs and they clearly weren't up and had just sent her through, typical of the neglectful parenting we have seen so many times.

Eight other guests came down at about 8.30, we served them tea, coffee, fruit cereal and I was cooking them all something when the mother whom we had briefly met the night before came through. She pretty much ignored her daughter, went to the edge of the kitchen which stands two steps above the Orangery and announced to all the other guests that, "Our other car is a Maserati too". I kid you not, this was her opening gambit. I processed what she had just said and was thinking of something appropriate to say when she headed out through the double doors to the garden where she duly lit up a cigarette. I think some of the other guests sniggered. Her daughter remained sat on the steps.

I went outside to ask if I could get her anything, a tea or coffee and what was her daughter allowed to have. "Oh, she can have anything," she replied. "A coffee for me would be lovely, thank you."

Her daughter had already helped herself to cereal earlier, perhaps we should have stopped her, but she had been down for quite a long time. Thank goodness she didn't have a major cornflake allergy although I imagine her mother would have been quite happy for me to take her to A&E. I took her mother, who had clearly had her lips plumped quite recently, a coffee, which she enjoyed along with the cigarette looking out over the views and her Maserati.

I served the rest of the guests with their breakfasts which they were just starting to enjoy when she came back in and leant against the door frame like Jessica Rabbit.

I asked if I could cook her some breakfast and she replied, "Oh no thank you, we had a box at The Derby on Thursday where we were entertaining friends. The food and champagne was flowing all day and we are still recovering, you know what it's like."

I don't think anyone could quite believe what they were hearing. She was clearly most annoyed when nobody enquired further. She then spent the next 45 minutes rotating between their room, the Orangery and the Terrace having more coffee and cigarettes. About 9.45, long after breakfast service was meant to be finished, her husband come down to breakfast apologising for being late. He then ordered full English and spent the next hour rotating between his breakfast and the terrace also smoking. All the while their daughter is completely ignored, and they hadn't brought any entertainment for her at all. Fortunately, Molly and Abbey the cat are always at hand to entertain so she was kept amused but nevertheless had to keep coming up to me in the kitchen for a chat and to see what I was doing.

A few hours later I was gardening when the girl came up to me all dressed for the wedding they were going to. Bored and inquisitive she started asking me every question under the sun. During a pause she then said, "That's not our car. Dad hired it for the weekend." Do you ever get those warm fuzzy feelings? I do.

Rolls Royce Man

One Saturday we were completely booked. Guests started arriving throughout the afternoon and were parking quite tidily. All the obvious parking spaces were taken. We received a phone call from the guests who were staying in the coach house that they would be late as they were having dinner out. At 9pm they pulled into the drive in an enormous new Rolls Royce. It was a very beautiful motor car. The driver could have pulled up outside the garage or parked tidily against the wall but instead parked diagonally across the drive meaning that nobody could get out or move their cars without asking the owner of the Rolls Royce to move. Also, there was no way any other vehicle could get into the drive and the driver could not have known if there were more guests due that evening.

I knew that all the guests were now in and didn't need to move their cars, so I didn't say anything knowing that this guest was clearly desperate for somebody in the morning to ask who owned the Rolls Royce. It was truly laughable. This group, the man, his wife, and a friend spent the whole stay just amongst themselves doing crosswords and didn't say a word to anyone. As it turned out, they were the first to leave so he never got the opportunity to tell anyone that this was his car.

Wedding Anniversary

One weekend Jane and I were both in the south east, Jane was visiting her father and I was playing in a sports tournament at Harrow. We were in two cars as our needs dictated. We knew we didn't have any guests arriving until Monday afternoon. I was due to return to Staffordshire on Sunday after the tournament whilst Jane was coming home with her father on the Monday.

At 4 o'clock on the Sunday afternoon I received a call from a couple who had arrived to find the house all locked up and nobody there. Naturally panic ensued. In our minds we did not have any bookings, but we are realists and accept that we can make mistakes. I was hugely apologetic, gave them the code for the front door and explained where their room was and to make themselves at home. I had forgotten that we had turned the heating off for the weekend because we were away.

I cut short what I was doing and jumped in the car wracked with guilt at the guests being confronted by an empty house and drove as fast as I dared. Fortunately, the traffic was light, and I made it back by 6.30. I pulled up next to a car in the drive and made my way up to the house. When I entered I could feel the chill. It was mid-February and Marlow House is a big property. I looked around for the guests, knocking on the door to their room but there was no answer. I hunted around the house but couldn't find them so naturally assumed that they had gone out for a walk. I nonchalantly walked into our private lounge to find an older couple sat on the sofa in their winter coats, gloves, scarves with our electric convector heater blowing out hot air between them.

To say that the ensuing conversation was difficult

would be an understatement. They told me that they had been here since 3pm were now frozen cold and that we had singularly ruined their wedding anniversary. I had no choice but to let them air all their grievances. I offered to make them some tea and scones, but they were belligerent, and I was at a loss as to how I was going to turn this situation around. It had crossed my mind that if they were so cold why hadn't they ventured out to one of our lovely pubs with a roaring fire, but I didn't think this was the appropriate time to ask what I thought was a very legitimate question.

I was wondering how I could get this clearly very unhappy couple out of our private space that was by now quite warm and into the guest lounge that was quite a few degrees cooler. I had immediately put the heating on, but it would take an hour or two to warm up. I felt I was on a hiding to nothing but nevertheless I had to try and find out their names and what had gone wrong with the booking.

I brought tea and scones through to our lounge, apologising profusely and then very gently asked for their names. They told me plainly that their daughter had booked it as a treat for their wedding anniversary which we had completely ruined. It was then that I had to tell them that the reservation was for tomorrow. I printed off the booking confirmation and the email conversations with their daughter. We had arranged to leave a card and a bottle of something for them. I told them that it wasn't a problem, they could have the room for tonight and it would be a pleasure to look after them but there was clearly no going back. The gentleman continued to tell me that it was all our fault and that we really had ruined their wedding anniversary. I tried to be as polite as possible but by now his embarrassment at their or their daughters' error was beyond repair. He could have backed down and apologised but instead continued to rail at me at which point he decided it was best that they leave which they duly did.

I sent an email to their daughter as soon as they had walked out of the door, but I never received a reply nor an apology. Fortunately for us this had been prepaid which softened the pain a little.

It's all our fault, naturally

One Saturday we were waiting for guests who were coming to attend a wedding. They had been in contact and I had given them the very simple directions to find us. Unfortunately, they also have that very nice lady inhabiting their satnav who can do no wrong. She took them on a lovely journey across Staffordshire taking in some wonderful views and some interesting driving experiences.

When they finally arrived, it was clear that they may have had a few words in the car. The wife felt it was completely appropriate to take everything out on me. From the moment I met them on the drive and offered to take their cases to the room she was telling me relentlessly that it was all our fault. To date she is the only guest who has rejected a room. I showed them into the four-poster room which arguably is our best, but she said that the mirrors were too high and there was no dressing table. I offered them another room which she showed equal disdain for but said it would do.

I took them up a glass of fizz and some of Jane's home-made sponge, the remedy for all ills. There was no thank you, but I didn't worry. Whenever we have difficult guests all I do is project myself 14 hours forwards knowing we will see the back of them and will probably never have to see them again.

I popped up again ten minutes later because I knew we would have to micro manage them. I asked if they were attending an event that evening, and they said they were going to the local venue to a wedding. I already knew this because I had pulled up the email conversation. I had asked them when they booked if they were attending an event and if they wanted a taxi booking because we are quite rural. Of course, this was in lines 2 and 3 of the email so I never received a reply as is usual.

I asked if they would like me to book them a taxi and they said yes. The taxi duly arrived but had to wait 30 minutes whilst she continued to get ready. As they left I said they should book the taxi home as soon as they arrived at the hotel as we are rural, and taxis come from town. I didn't get much of a reply. I had discussed with them and demonstrated the door locks and the code as they left but I could tell they weren't interested and had more pressing things to think about.

Jane and I knew things would probably get worse because it is a law that when something goes wrong, everything goes wrong. I just felt that this was one evening to stay up and wait for them to get home.

As already mentioned elsewhere, the local wedding venue is licensed until midnight, so most guests arrive home by 12.30am.

12.30am came and went. I had a cup of tea at 1am and was pleasantly surprised to find quite a compelling choice on the television. By 2am however it was getting quite tiring when I heard the inevitable prodding and unsuccessful beeping of the security keypad. The door was then rattled very hard in some mad endeavour to force it open and then voices were raised.

I opened the door to find the couple there in a state of mild distress. "Everything OK?" I asked expecting an apology for coming in at 2am having forgotten the code that I meticulously went through with them on their departure.

I was then subjected to yet another tirade of how when they wanted to come home at 11pm because they had had enough they couldn't get a taxi and were disappointed to find they would have to wait 90 minutes because it was a busy Saturday night. When the taxi did arrive, it was late at 12.50am and almost everyone had left or gone to bed. The taxi driver then took them on a wild goose chase because the lady in his satnav told him where to go (we are 3 miles away from the venue on a straight road). He took 70 minutes to get them home and charged them £30. Apparently, it was all my fault again, for living in the country, being impossible to find, being too dark in the countryside. They went off to bed.

The following morning as we were preparing breakfast they came down quite early, she was fuming again and told me that she had left her iPad on the back seat of the taxi and that the whole weekend was a disaster and that she wished she had never come to Staffordshire or Marlow House.

I told her to try and relax that I would call the taxi company and try to locate her iPad, "sit down, have a cup of tea and I will cook you something delicious." No sign of a thank you, I was just thankful that she calmed down a bit although she insisted on regaling everything to the other guests. After a few phone calls, I found out who her taxi driver was. He wasn't starting his next shift for 45 minutes, but his Control Manager said he would get in touch which he duly did, the iPad was located, and we arranged for it to be brought over. Not a word of thanks from the couple just more moaning. To say that we were glad to see the back of them would have been an understatement. However, two days later we did have an email of apology from her saying that in hindsight she realised that none of it was our fault and to thank us for locating her iPad, so some sense of reason and normality must have finally entered their unbelievably selfish lives.

Not all my guest stories are about nightmare guests, we have had some wonderful people stay who deserve a mention.

Some people just make you glad to be alive

We were hosting a pre-wedding family event for a lovely couple. His parents had flown in from Trinidad and Tobago and were some of the most wonderfully warm hearted and positive people you could ever have the good fortune to meet. He worked for the UN and oversaw the disaster relief in Haiti? He told us stories of the disaster when it struck and the humanitarian efforts afterwards, how the people pulled together and his very small part in (he was a very humble man) the unfolding drama. He and his wife were so full of life, despite having had a long journey from the Caribbean into Heathrow and up to Staffordshire, they wanted to engage in everything. They had something to eat and then they wanted to dance and show us their customs from Trinidad and Tobago, they were so warm and enthusiastic and all this even though he was completely blind. When we consider some of the demanding and whingeing people we have had come across our threshold, this man was a breath of fresh air and it reflected on his son who was also thoroughly delightful.

The Painful Breakfast Guest

We recently had two business travellers staying from Yorkshire. They each had a room and went out in the evening to have dinner with clients. They said that they needed to leave early and therefore weren't too worried about breakfast. We naturally told them that it wasn't an issue for us to get up and make them breakfast (after all that is what they have paid for) so it was agreed that they would come down for breakfast at 7am. Our alarm goes off at 6.30 to give us 30 minutes to get dressed, lay the table, organise all the breakfast ingredients, cereals, yoghurts, prepare the fresh fruit etc. He comes down at 6.40 bright as a button, an enormous man with an enormous voice and proceeds to wax lyrical about the virtues of his home county whilst standing in our kitchen. He then wants to discuss "Four in a Bed" and how hard it must be to run a BnB. And so on, pontificating and generally being annoying. It's bad enough at the best of times but at 6.40am when we are trying to get breakfast organised it is very painful. And yet he was blissfully unaware that we were trying to get on and do a job, so we made him tea and toast in the interim which he proceeded to consume whilst stood next to us as we worked. There are times when I wish I could reciprocate. But on second thoughts ...

Wedding guest

We had a lady stay recently who was going to a wedding as a single guest. She arrived at four in the afternoon and was due at the wedding in the evening. Another couple staying was also going to the wedding and wanted a taxi as did this other lady. I offered to take them there, so they could just get a taxi back. We agreed to go at 7.30pm. I knocked on the door of the single lady to explain that I was taking the other couple at 7.30 (it was now 7pm) but she declined the lift and said she would get a taxi. This was a Tuesday evening and as I pointed out, we are quite rural. I went and told the other couple that she had declined but suggested to the lady that she might go and ask as it seemed to make such sense. She did and returned to say that she was going to come with us at 7.30. The young couple came down at 7.20. She looked lovely; he looked as though he was due in court - not really, just my little joke. They asked for a drink which we duly gave them. 7.30 came and went, as did 7.45. At 8pm the single lady finally came down. She had been staying with us for four hours, had been offered a *gratis* lift and yet came down half an hour late making the young couple late and had me hanging around for an extra half an hour. No apology, absolutely nothing. Quite extraordinary.

The Dullards of Doncaster

We had a family of four who came to stay in the Coach House on one occasion. I met them in the car park with Molly and immediately introduced myself and Molly and welcomed them to Marlow House. None of them said hello. The children were clearly nervous of Molly. I offered to carry their bags for them, picked up two and waited whilst they got themselves organised. They weren't as bad as some other guests for whom I have stood there waiting for ten minutes to sort themselves out. They followed me into the house and through to the Coach House. They still hadn't said a word at this point. We barely saw them again until breakfast. They came through without saying a word. I asked if they would like tea or coffee. The mother said, tea. Nobody else said anything. When I asked if I could cook them anything, the mother ordered something for her and her partner and said the children were fine with cereal. They finished breakfast and left. Having pre-paid online the only words we heard any of them utter during the entire stay were:

"Tea please" and "poached eggs on toast for me, full English for him, the children are fine with cereal."

This family could have been very painful but they didn't loiter in silence, so it wasn't too bad. One of the great difficulties owners of BnBs can have is with incredibly dull people. Jane tells me that is more about me than the guests. I don't feel compelled to know everything about everyone who comes to stay but it is a reward of the job to engage in some stimulating conversation. I understand that we can't all be erudite, well read, conversationally gifted and entertaining but some basic interests and a desire to get on with your fellow man is a good start. Most of our guests are lovely, I am not disputing that but there are some that are so dull they suck the life out of a room. It is always our job to remain professional and courteous and I would like to think that we have become very adept at this, but it can be difficult sometimes. We have guests, and it is the same with other people we know generally, who will tell you everything about their lives, absolutely exhausting their annual word allowance but will not once ask anything about us. It reminds me of that great line, "Well, that's enough about me, what do you think about me?"

Please don't get me wrong, we have no urgent need to tell anyone else about ourselves, that is not the point, it's just that we find people who relentlessly talk about themselves so excruciatingly dull.

Hagrid

I am terrible. I know this, Jane constantly tells me so, but I can't help it. For as long as I can remember I have had to instantly give certain people a nickname. Not everyone, not everyone can justify a nickname or deserve one. I was always very disappointed at school by never having a nickname. I don't mean an abbreviation or a standard nickname like Chalky or Nobby but a genuine nickname that reflected a trait, aptitude, or fondness. Of course, there are some nicknames that none of us would ever want, stinky or psycho (even that's borderline) but some nicknames are just plain great. I have given people nicknames that have just stuck, to the point that most people then call them that. This slightly unusual trait has spilt over into the BnB. We meet over 1000 people a year at the BnB so it is to be expected. I probably only give one in a hundred a nickname, after all most of our guests aren't with us long enough to get to know them to give them a nickname but others just immediately slot into a particular moniker.

A couple of years ago a couple came to stay. We looked out as they alighted from their car and I turned to Jane and said, "Hagrid's arrived". This wasn't so much a nickname as stating the obvious. This guest was the biggest human being I have ever seen in person. Fortunately, they were the second guests to arrive, so we had an opportunity to move some rooms around. Marlow House is a large Victorian rectory but even we have some restricted spaces. We moved them from our white room that has a toilet area a little better suited to the slimmer build, to The Cedar room which is huge. I met them in the car park and was immediately transfixed not only by his sheer size but by the arrangement of his teeth which were quite extraordinary; like an uncompleted Tetris. They were certainly pleasant enough people and we didn't think anything more until the following morning when Jane shouted at me to come out to the hall. Water was pouring down through the ceiling. I immediately thought we must have a burst pipe but couldn't understand why considering it was mid-July. I worked out that the bathroom to the Cedar room was directly above. I ran upstairs and heard the shower going and somebody in there. Decisions, decisions. I said nothing and ran downstairs where Jane had already pre-empted me and put some buckets down to catch the water. In time it subsided, and I realised it had leaked whilst the shower was on. It was only after they had checked out and I could get in to see what the problem was that I realised his enormous frame and weight had made the shower tray push down so far that the silicone seal had torn itself from the tray and the water had got in behind. It wasn't an enormous job to remove the seal and re-do it, but it had been quite a surprise.

The biggest surprise is that this gentleman did not mention before arriving that he was a man mountain. I would have thought there must be so many instances where he would have been restricted from doing certain things due to a building design. I think I would have always mentioned it before going somewhere. If you should ever happen to sit next to man on a flight who is as big as the plane and had his teeth repaired by a visually impaired dentist, you know you are sitting next to Hagrid.

Why would you?

We think Marlow House is very nice, well we would. It is set in the beautiful Staffordshire countryside with spectacular views as already mentioned a few times. People tend to stay with us because they are going to an event or because they want to be in the countryside. There is another very small group of people who just feel that they need to get away and have some quiet time to themselves in order to unwind. These generally tend to be Londoners, stressed and exhausted and all they want is somewhere quiet where they can sleep and unwind until work starts again on Monday. I can completely understand this, we see people trapped on a treadmill unable to get off who just need to try and relax. We used to see this years ago when we went on holiday in Asia to Malaysia or Thailand (I used to travel there on business years ago). Professional couples from banking, finance, law and other high-powered professions would take a very expensive villa within a five star hotel and sleep all day, take their meals in their private house and just recuperate so they could go back to their very stressful jobs that enabled them to earn enough money to rent a very expensive villa in a five star hotel. We thought they were bonkers even then.

Now in our little BnB we see couples who need to de-stress for the weekend and we totally get it. What we just don't get is why they would struggle through the London traffic and the M25 and M40 on a Friday night to go somewhere 140 miles away when they could just get the train to East Sussex? They then have a not quite so arduous and lengthy journey back on the Sunday. In many instances they have even had to hire a car as car ownership is no longer mainstream for Londoners. Please do not get me wrong, they are very welcome, and we hope they continue to come but we hardly see them. We had one couple who didn't make it down for breakfast on either morning. One entire day they did not leave the room at all and just ate some things they had picked up at M&S on the way up. On the Sunday morning they took Molly for a 30 minute walk around the lanes and then waxed lyrical about how clean the air was and how they would love to live in the country. They then went back to their room for four hours. I think they had a good time.

Hyacinth Bucket

Another lady who immediately suffered the ignominy of my nicknaming was Hyacinth Bucket and her husband. She was a caricature of the television character who was already a caricature of certain people who are social climbers. Although we have had many guests who have certain aspirations she is the only one to date to have picked up this moniker. We had two days of complete hilarity and couldn't wait to hear the next thing she might say. To this day we wonder if she was doing it for laughs. The thing we most remember was her husband who really was like the downtrodden husband from the television program. She told us in great details about his heart condition and how she was great friends with his surgeon and cardiologist. Both mornings he had huge English breakfasts and asked for his eggs to be fried and his bacon well done. It was very funny.

Tintin, the MG and Miss Drippy

One weekend we had a lovely MGB pull into the drive and a young couple in their late twenties got out. He was genuinely dressed like TinTin, and even had a similar haircut. We were waiting for Snowy the dog to get out or be followed up the drive by Captain Haddock. His girlfriend was a plain girl who clearly wasn't in on the whole Tintin thing. He spoke for her for most of the weekend even ordering her breakfast for her, she didn't really get a chance to express herself at all and came across as very drippy which probably suited him as he was clearly very OCD. He spent far more time covering up the MGB and polishing it than he did taking any notice of his girlfriend. I wonder if they are still together?

When the waters break

We had a lovely couple who came to stay who were going to a wedding which seemed very brave considering she was very heavily pregnant with twins. That night her waters broke, and they rushed off to hospital in town a long way from where they lived where the twins were born. We found a note in the morning telling us what had happened although we could have guessed as the waters broke in the bed which had to be dried out then cleaned. We are hugely sympathetic to these things happening and of course we are so pleased that the birth went well but we didn't get any kind of offer to have the mattress cleaned. They were a lovely young couple but like most people, seemed to think that part of our remit is just to clear up after everyone else.

Can we have a bigger bed?

Our Salle Gris or grey room is our most popular room. It is very large with a big bay window that looks out over our gardens, the valley and looks through our wonderful Cedar trees. It really is a lovely bright room and in it we have put a king-size four poster bed because the room is big enough to carry it. We had a couple of guests who, when they reviewed their stay thought we could have had a bigger bed in the room. Managing people's expectations is always tricky but sometimes we know we just can't please everyone.

How big is your dog?

We try and do the best we can for our guests. If they give us their parameters, we will try and match them and provide the best stay that we can. We don't want to be restrictive but sometimes we must be. For example, we acknowledge that some people have allergies to animals especially dogs and cats therefore we don't allow dogs upstairs in the main house to keep it as free as possible for those with allergies. We do however allow dogs to stay in the coach house downstairs and hope that guests respect this.

We had a lady who booked to stay and said she had two small dogs if that would be OK. We said that would be fine but that the dogs couldn't come through to the breakfast area. She agreed and said they would be no trouble at all. When she arrived and opened the boot of the car two enormous huskies jumped out. Huskies are designed to run, they love exercise and want to be outside, they are also huge. Her dogs were no exception to the species and they were chomping at the bit to have a run around. When they came into the house they absolutely filled up the hallway. I was wondering what this lady would consider to be large dogs having described these as small. It was clear that what they needed was a very long and energetic walk but clearly this didn't fit in with the owner's agenda, so she took them down to our tennis court to throw a ball for them. We were concerned that they would be rampant in the coach house but as it happened they were fine. After they checked out the next day we went down to the tennis court to find that she had just left all their excrement all over the court from the evening before and then again in the morning, once again we are staggered at what guests think is our responsibility and not theirs.

Looking for a freebie

The hotel industry is awash with stories of guests who make life very difficult for the owners and then try and blackmail them by threatening to leave a dreadful review. We have never experienced this although we did have one couple who complained that the bed was uncomfortable. We have received so many written reviews as well as verbal comments about how comfortable our beds are. With over 3000 guests this was the only time anyone has ever said they were uncomfortable. When they told me, I apologised and explained that generally everyone sleeps well at Marlow House. They wouldn't let it go so I put the ball in their court and asked what they would like us to do about it. They said that if they come again they wanted a free night. I thought this was quite extraordinary because I would have thought if the problem was that the bed was uncomfortable and spoilt their stay then the last thing they would have wanted was to come and stay again and have another uncomfortable night's sleep. Fortunately, this is the only time this has ever happened. We never saw them again.

Unrealistic Expectations

Recently we had a couple who arrived very late and were going to a wedding. They rushed in, and up to their room in a panic. I thought it best to pop my head in and ask how they were planning on getting to the wedding. They said they wanted to call a taxi. I gazed out of the window at the range of hills, the sheep and the pastoral elegance of our surroundings, waited a moment for comedic timing and asked, "What time would you like it for?"

"We need it now," they replied.

"I don't think you will get a taxi here that quickly, did you not book one from the list I sent you by email?"

"What email?"

Selfish guests

We had returning guests coming to stay for three nights. They had responded to one of our emails where we give guests who have visited before a special deal. In this instance it was a three-night stay including cream tea, dinner and other treats. They had booked a few months in advance, so it is always possible that things may come up in the meantime.

Unfortunately, quite close to their arrival, Jane's aunt sadly passed away and the funeral was arranged for the Tuesday that this couple were arriving. We emailed them to let them know and gave them the codes to the front door and explained that they were in the same four poster room that they had stayed in previously, that we couldn't be there due to the funeral, but Molly would be there to greet them, to make themselves at home and we would be back as soon as possible.

We had the funeral and naturally joined the family and friends for something to eat and drink afterwards. We stayed as long as we could but knew that we had to get back, leaving Essex at 3.30 and arriving back in Staffordshire at 6.30.

When we walked in after a long drive they were most put out that we hadn't been there to greet them, especially the lady. Even after tea and cake she didn't feel any reason to apologise for her behaviour and continued to be very difficult. We had looked after them on two previous occasions and built up some rapport. Quite extraordinary. The following morning, she was as nice as pie but didn't mention anything about the previous day.

Yet another funeral

We had another occasion that centred around a funeral. It really is incredibly inconvenient for our guests when someone dies. Jane was away and inconsiderately a friend of mine had passed away. Naturally I was attending the funeral. Our lovely lady at the time, Sharon, who is supremely organised and incredibly efficient was here to meet and greet the guests since I was very aware of what happened previously when we were not there to meet and greet because of a funeral.

The guests got off to a bad start by getting lost, of course they chose not to read the email with the directions on. When they eventually arrived at Marlow House they came to the rear of the house. Knocking on our next-door neighbour's cottage which had the house name "Little Corner Cottage" right by the door he was knocking on, the door was answered by our super friendly neighbour, Jan. Unbelievably with suitcases in hand he marched straight past her and into their house putting his case down in their kitchen. A discussion then commenced where he was very rude to our neighbours complaining about the journey, signage etc and upsetting Jan. When Jan was finally able to get a word in, she pointed out his error. She thought he was expecting her to put his cases back in the car. Reluctantly he repacked his car and drove the 50 yards down the lane to the entrance to Marlow House.

There he met Sharon who really does not suffer fools, especially rude ones. Not being there, I don't know exactly how the discourse developed but I can imagine. Despite what was probably a very difficult encounter, Sharon being a consummate professional, served them both a cream tea out on the terrace with our beautiful views which can relax and calm down the most stressed of people. We always felt that huge global difficulties could be more easily negotiated over a lovely cup of tea on our terrace with views out across the valley.

When I returned just after six o'clock, I met this 'gentleman' (in the loosest sense of the term) and his wife. Of all the things that he could have said to me, I nearly fell over when his opening gambit was, "Did you really need to go to the funeral?" It was wrong on so many levels but from his own perspective, he knew I was about to cook them both dinner. I would have thought that it really wasn't worth being difficult and confrontational at that point.

Here at Marlow House our aim primarily is to ensure that all our guests have a wonderful experience however difficult they are. We would never want to sink as low and behave as badly as some of our guests. I must reiterate that those who have been truly awful and completely disappointing as *Homo Sapiens* are so very rare, almost everyone is lovely.

By the time they had digested their scallops followed by *beouf bourguinon*, white chocolate torte, cheese, coffee and treats they calmed down and were bordering on reasonable, much like the advert for Snickers. Perhaps that's what it is, people become Divas when they are hungry. In which case carry a little snack with you, so you don't have to come across as a complete idiot.

Private DJ

We recently had a lovely group who came to stay to celebrate their combined 25th wedding anniversaries. They asked us to cook them a special supper and they settled in for a lovely evening. We have an iPod docking station as well as a Bluetooth speaker and we ask the guests if they want to put on their own music. About 10 o'clock in the evening one of the ladies came up to me to ask if I could help her connect her phone to the Bluetooth speaker which I duly did. She then said that she didn't really know how to get her music to play so I took her phone and set it up for her. In doing so I connected everything and started playing the first song that came up to show that it was all connected and that she could now scroll through and play whatever song she wanted.

I didn't have to do all this, but we like to go the extra mile and if that means sorting out a guest's own private technology then we will do whatever we can to make our guests' experience as good as possible.

I thought she was going to say, "Thank you very much for all your help, that is so kind of you.". Imagine my surprise when she said, "That wasn't the song I wanted."

You let yourselves down

I had a midweek couple who stayed for one night. Jane was away visiting her father. The couple were very dull and uncommunicative, I could also tell they were more than a little OCD. When they came to leave, I was seeing them off at the front door. I asked if they had had an enjoyable stay. They said that the house was beautiful with spectacular views and that they had enjoyed their stay but "the room was dirty." He then actually said, "You have let your business and yourselves down.". I never imagined for one moment that anyone ever actually said that. They then departed. I was crestfallen. I immediately went to the room to have a good look round. In fairness, I did spot a cobweb in the corner of the ceiling, it was March so not that unusual, they can turn up overnight. I was so shocked that I Googled where they live. Their house was on the market for sale, so I could see all the images of their rooms. They were completely barren with literally just a bed, or a couple of chairs and everything was bright white. They themselves were super minimalist so I convinced myself that they were just crazy people but as I always say everything is about perspective and perhaps from their point of view the room was dirty.

Coffee Machine Lady

There was a lovely group of ten people staying organised by a returning guest. As a collective, the whole group was delightful, they had just come to have a good time and there was no edge to them at all and everyone was appreciative but there was one lady amongst them who was not as friendly as the others, struggling to say a thank you for anything. In fact, when they came to leave the other nine made such a point of saying goodbyes and expressing how much they had enjoyed themselves whilst this lady was the first to get in the car and said nothing. That's fine, she wasn't difficult although she did seem to have most of the food issues. We certainly didn't mind, after all, each to their own. However, at breakfast on the first morning as I asked everyone if they would like tea or coffee, this lady asked for de-caffeinated coffee. Not a problem. She then asked what make the de-caffeinated coffee was. We tend to carry a very wide range of coffees and teas, probably twenty in all but sadly we don't offer a choice in the brand of de-caffeinated coffee. I told her that is was Arabica beans and the brand name. She then rather haughtily said, “I have my own coffee machine at home.”. I asked her if she would like the de-caffeinated coffee to which she replied, “No thank you, I will have tea.” After a few more questions she settled for decaffeinated Earl Grey. It would probably have been easier if she had brought her own coffee machine with her from home. By the way we have a coffee machine, but it clearly wouldn't have been good enough. I did wonder how the conversation would go if she calls in to a Costa/Starbucks/Nero (other coffee brands are available).

The Money Grabbers

From time to time we have run some special promotions with companies like Secret Escapes, Voyage Prive and others. This is usually during the quiet January - March period. One year we ran the promotion and it went quite well. As part of the deal we included dinner at Marlow House for one of the evenings. Secret Escapes oversaw the phrasing and we successfully sold 58 two and three night deals. All of these were very straightforward except for one couple who argued the semantics of the phrasing with Secret Escapes and insisted that there wasn't enough clarity and that the deal implied dinner on two nights. The other 57 people who booked didn't raise this, but this one couple did and absolutely dug their heels in. Secret Escapes then had to pay us for the extra night's dinner. When the couple arrived we already had a pretty good idea what they were like from our discussion with our contact at Secret Escapes. Fortunately, the way the bookings worked they ate alone both evenings but at breakfast they were very happy to regale to the table how successful they had been in pulling Secret Escapes up on their phraseology. They then proceeded to boast about all the cruises they had been on, were going on and all the amazing deals you can get if you are tenacious enough. They were thoroughly dreadful, and we were very happy to see them leave.

The body's not even cold yet

Another couple led to a very strange and quite unpleasant experience. In fairness she was OK, but her husband was one of those people you hope never to meet again. Within a short space of arriving he had told us that his mother had recently passed away. Naturally we were sympathetic. He then started going on about his brother and his mother's estate. His brother wanted to hold on to his mother's house for sympathetic reasons but the chap staying with us clearly had both eyes firmly on the money. I made the mistake of expressing an interest in his dilemma. He then spent every waking moment pressing me as to what he could do to force a sale and get hold of the money. I have met some greedy, avaricious people in my time, but this chap was quite extraordinary, and his mother had only passed away the week before. His wife didn't say very much at all, probably through embarrassment. It was all I could do to hold back from telling this chap to get a grip on reality. Another car that I was very pleased to see going out of the drive.

Supremely irritating guests

A couple from Yorkshire, which is never a good start, came to stay as she was having a throat operation here at our local hospital which apparently is a centre of excellence for that type of surgery. We thought she was having an operation to remove her inflated sense of self-importance. It really was like having Hyacinth Bucket to stay. Although the lady didn't pick holes in everything, she always had something to say about everything here at Marlow House in between telling us how wonderful her life was and how amazing her children were. We heard everything, she barely came up for breath. It made me realise how small and inconspicuous my own life was compared to her multi-faceted international lifestyle. She did of course make the mistake of filling in her guest form so we were able to corroborate her extraordinary life with the reality on Google. Was she the most irritating guest we have ever had to stay? No, for that crowning glory we must turn to the couple from Faversham.

The Couple from Faversham

We really have no idea why they came to stay with us.

They bought a Secret Escapes offer but when you consider how far Stafford is from Faversham on the Kent coast it was hardly an economically wise choice although hopefully they had read the lovely reviews our previous kind guests had left and therefore felt compelled to visit us here at Marlow House.

They were both so loud mouthed it was truly painful. Not content with always being quite a few decibels above all our other guests they also felt compelled to tell us and everyone else about their truly amazing life in a relentless tirade. She managed to move from the cruise down the Nile to the holiday in Florida to the trip to Bali in a seamless flourish barely stopping for breath, this house, that investment, her wonderful son, incredible grandchildren, it went on and on and on and on. This lady never knew when to shut up and as her voice faltered after 29 hours of relentless boasting her husband stepped in to take up the slack. It wasn't until the following day that they released everyone's straps and allowed them to go, once they had signed the declaration that they had been in the presence of the most gifted and talented people in Christendom. To this day the relentless whining of her voice wakes me up in the night screaming and with a cold sweat.

Wedding guests

The ten-year-old organised them all

There was a time when we used to have a lot of wedding groups and wedding guests. The thing that we found as a rule of thumb was that the brides were pretty switched on, but their maids of honour were utterly hapless. However, we did have one wedding group constituting ten girls including the bride, mother, mother in law, sisters, best friends and the bride’s ten-year-old daughter. Thank goodness for the ten-year-old as she was the only one with any common sense at all. The group were truly hopeless and seemed incapable of doing anything of their own volition but the ten-year-old managed to organise them all and get them to the wedding on time. Thank goodness for youth!

Guests beware

We have had so many guests over the years who have tried to portray an image of wealth or success. Some guests will arrive in a big car with private number plates, others will come to breakfast draped in jewellery, some will wax lyrical about their amazing home and some will even allude to how successful or wealthy they are quite directly. Sometimes it is so blatant and awful it is embarrassing. The thing that I should tell all guests who visit hotels and BnBs is that when you fill in your form we get to see your address and Google Earth and Rightmove allow us into your home. It isn't very often I waste a few minutes of my life looking these things up but if you choose to make an idiot of yourself with unnecessary boasts I might be inclined to look you up. It can sometimes be quite surprising and occasionally very different to the image portrayed. I doubt I am the only hotelier to do this. That's the problem with the internet and open source, there are no more secrets. So be careful what you boast about.

In the moving house business

We had one couple from London who managed to take the whole house prices thing to another level. As per normal they were dominating the breakfast conversation talking about property prices in London. To make conversation and hoping to move it away from London property, to save the embarrassment of our other guests I asked the lady what she did for a living. She replied, "I am in the moving house business". I said that I didn't know what that was, that I had never heard of it before. She said that she looks out for all the Ofsted reports and keeps an eye on local property prices talking to agents all the time and when they can see the next up and coming streets they move, usually no more than three or four streets away. I remarked that this was a very unusual business. She replied with great candour and feigned modesty that the last move two years ago made them £500,000 and the next one probably would too, that it pays for school fees, holidays and a great life and was very tax efficient too.

You must admire her resourcefulness and her ability to spot the opportunity, but it makes a mockery of meritocracy. As I write this, property prices in London seem to be going into reverse, but it seems like she made hay while the sun was shining.

Encapsulating it all

One weekend we had a young lady in her late twenties who was an artist from London come to stay. She called us to ask where we were and said she would be with us between six and seven. We had subsequent phone calls during the evening and she finally arrived at 11pm. She was delayed because she had spent five hours trying to find a fascinator. She came down for breakfast at 9.45 then announced she was vegan or something. She was due to leave for the wedding by one o'clock but set off at two o'clock and seemed to be wearing everything that she had brought with her. She would have walked in during the ceremony. The following morning, she came down to breakfast with someone she had met at the wedding who had then stayed over, and he just came and sat down for breakfast. They then proceeded to sit there for about two hours. She checked out but telephoned the next day to say that she had left her phone charger with us. We found it, posted it to her. The day it arrived she rang to say that she had also left her Mac charger with us which we also found under the bed. Not having offered to pay us for any of the postage we asked for £5. She never sent it to us, so we never sent her the charger. We weren't being mean but this girl had been so difficult and demanding. I am trying to think where she came from, hmm let me see ...

CHAPTER 13
THE ADVANTAGES OF RUNNING A BnB

Being Your Own Boss

In yet another survey, probably completely made up, researchers found that 90% of people working for someone would rather be doing something else, with a majority wishing they could work for themselves. If this really was the case, we would have millions of wannabe entrepreneurs. There is a big reality gap between wanting to run your own business, prising yourself away from that monthly pay cheque and the benefits of corporate life into the big unknown of developing your own marketplace, product and seeing it through, turning it into positive cash flow and hopefully self-sufficiency. On the face of it, there are so many obstacles and so much uncertainty which is why only one in 6 work for themselves leaving 5 in 6 or twenty five million people collecting a cheque at the end of the month from their employers.

It is a great feeling being your own boss and being in command of your own destiny but do not be under any illusions, you will still ultimately be answerable to your customers, after all it is they who pay your bills. However, as the owner you can dictate when you are open and how many guests you want to have. You can also run the BnB exactly how you want although I would suggest that you do this with one eye firmly on what your customers want too.

No More Commuting

Because the BnB is generally also your own home, gone

would be the days of commuting. All those wasted hours travelling to and from your place of work and the costs involved all of which are paid for out of taxed income. It might not seem that big a deal but when you really calculate how much of your life you spend travelling to and from work it can really add up. It was certainly a big thing for me as I had previously driven 30,000 miles a year in previous businesses.

Tax Efficiency

Running a BnB is a most unusually tax efficient business because you are using your own home for business. Almost all the costs of running the business and therefore your home come out before tax is due as opposed to all your income being taxed at source as an employee. On the downside though, if after three years of trading as a BnB, to sell the business as a going concern you would have to pay capital gains tax whereas as a private home there would be no tax to pay. It is important to understand this before embarking on the business and you should get a good understanding of any tax implications from your accountant or financial advisor.

Watch out for the VAT

One of the considerations when working on your business plan is to consider if it is financially viable and financially efficient. I stated early on that it will not make you rich but will give you a very comfortable life and a very nice lifestyle. You should consider that under current UK tax law, you can only trade to £82,000 each year without being liable for VAT. This is the tax that the UK Government puts on almost all sales and at the time of writing it is 20%. The level at which any business must pay VAT is £82,000. This means that if you trade at £83,000 in one 12-month period you will become liable for VAT going forwards. When you start your BnB you have no turnover and as each month progresses you begin to build your turnover.

It is your responsibility therefore to keep a "running total" of your gross turnover and when it cumulatively reaches £82,000 then you need to inform the VAT office and register. This does not mean you owe VAT retrospectively; from henceforth you will have to pay 20% on all your turnover even if it drops back below £82,000 in which case you would have to de-register or fill in a 'zero' in the VAT due box in your quarterly return and run the risk of instigating a visit by an HMRC official.

If you have reached £83,000 that means that going forwards you will have to pay 20% or £16,600 to the VAT office. From this figure you can claim back VAT that you have paid on any goods and services required in running the BnB. Unfortunately, most foodstuffs do not attract VAT so there are very few things that a BnB can regularly claim the VAT back from. That is a sizeable amount from your income suddenly gone leaving you now with a gross income of about £69,000.

You could elect to add VAT to your rates but that would make the room rate £120 instead of £100 and there will be plenty of other hotels and BnBs not registered for VAT who will be a lot cheaper. Unfortunately to make registering for VAT work for a BnB or small business you must lift your turnover to something close to £140,000 to make it worthwhile which is a huge uplift in trade and, critically, workload. This means you would need to have at least 4 bedrooms, possibly five so the whole proposal morphs into something completely different. You may well find you have to take on a full-time staff member when the business grows to that size as well.

It really is a big consideration which is why many BnBs stop working part of the way through the year just to avoid the dilemma of registering for VAT and everything that comes with that decision choosing not to work for three or four months in order to remain below the VAT threshold. It does seem a crazy system although larger hotels will argue that they are at a disadvantage to smaller

BnBs as they will have to charge VAT on their rooms. It is a big consideration when developing your business plan.

CHAPTER 14
AFTER ALL THAT, DO YOU STILL WANT TO RUN A BnB?

Guests are like fish, they begin to smell after three days
Benjamin Franklin

What conclusions have you drawn? We can only speak for ourselves when we say that we have really enjoyed running our Bed and Breakfast. We made some mistakes - like our early marketing - but we couldn't have known at the time. Cooking evening meals was by far the biggest mistake, a lot of work for little reward but we did get to spend some quality time with guests as we often ate with them and some have become good friends so there was an upside.

How do we feel about the BnB after five years? We still enjoy it enormously, but I must admit that we have changed our business model quite dramatically and do a lot less than we used to do which suits us better.

It is not an endeavour to embark on lightly. It is a very hard thing to do as a single person, but some people don't have any other option. If you have a property suitable to be a BnB that isn't going to cost a lot of money to convert and you have the drive and energy, then we would heartily recommend you have a go.

If you don't like having strangers in your house, then don't even consider it!

Printed in Great Britain
by Amazon

33188316R00095